# Now I Lay Me Down to Sleep...

## *drawing nearer to* God *with your dreams*

To my friend, Sandy,
May you be
blessed by reading
my book and
may God draw
near to you.
Sweet dreams,
Gloria

2012

# Now I Lay Me Down to Sleep...

## *drawing nearer to God with your dreams*

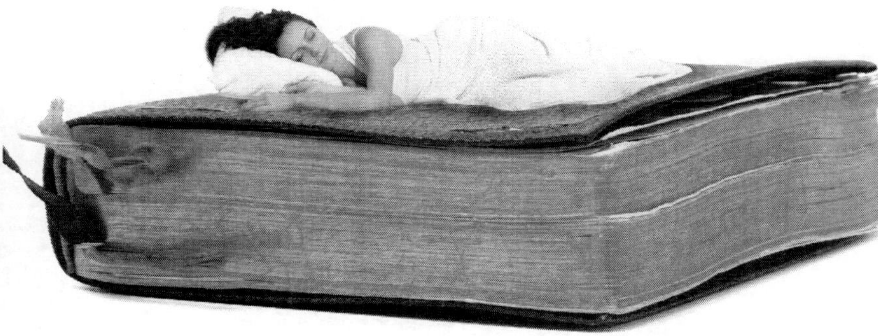

GLORIA FISHER

TATE PUBLISHING
AND ENTERPRISES, LLC

*Now I Lay Me Down to Sleep*


Published by Tate Publishing & Enterprises, LLC

127 E. Trade Center Terrace | Mustang, Oklahoma 73064 USA
1.888.361.9473 | www.tatepublishing.com

Tate Publishing is committed to excellence in the publishing industry. The company reflects the philosophy established by the founders, based on Psalm 68:11,

*"The Lord gave the word and great was the company of those who published it."*


*Cover design by Kenna Davis*
*Interior design by Lauro Talibong*

Published in the United States of America

ISBN: 978-1-62147-228-5
1. Body, Mind & Spirit / Dreams
2. Religion / Christian Life / Personal Growth
12.09.14

# Dedication

To the Giver of dreams

# Acknowledgment

I would like to express a special thank you to three people who helped make this book possible: To my beloved husband, Bill, who trusts God enough to put me into His hands for Him to have His way with me, who listens patiently as I relate my dreams, and who believes God speaks to me. To my son, Chris, who kept encouraging me to get to work. To Dr. Bob Glaze who saved my life and believed I could do anything.

> "Draw near to God and He will draw near to you."
>
> James 4:8 (RSV)

# Contents

Chapter 1: Understanding Your Dream's Language ..................... 13
- What Is a Dream? ..................... 15
- How Often Do You Dream? ..................... 19
- Holding Onto Your Dreams ..................... 20
- Tell Me What They Look Like ..................... 25
- What Do Dreams Sound Like? ..................... 30
- What If You Don't Dream? ..................... 31
- What is the Purpose of Dreams? ..................... 32

Chapter 2: Knowing Your Dream Type ..................... 35
- A Promise Dream ..................... 36
- A Warning Dream ..................... 37
- A Blessing Dream ..................... 39
- Numinous Dreams ..................... 40
- A Prophetic Dream ..................... 41
- A Teaching Dream ..................... 42
- A Comforting Dream ..................... 43
- A Healing Dream ..................... 44
- Two Helping Dreams ..................... 45
- A Correcting Dream ..................... 46
- An Encouraging Dream ..................... 47
- A Problem-solving Dream ..................... 48
- A Directing Dream ..................... 49
- Giving of a Ministry Dream ..................... 52
- A Turning Point Dream ..................... 53
- Conclusion ..................... 54

Chapter 3: Dream Journaling ..................... 57
Treating Your Dreams with Respect? ..................... 58
What Is a Dream Journal? ..................... 59
What Is Your Style of Dream Journal? ..................... 60
Using Interpretation Sheets to Understand Your Dreams ..................... 62
Blank Interpretation Sheet ..................... 63
Joseph's Dream on an Interpretation Sheet ..................... 67
What Does a Dream Journal Look Like? ..................... 68
What Are the Benefits of a Dream Journal? ..................... 74

Chapter 4: How People In the Bible Used Their Dreams to Draw Nearer to God ..................... 77
Jacob ..................... 78
Joseph ..................... 81
Daniel ..................... 84
Joseph, the Husband of Mary ..................... 87
Gideon ..................... 89
Solomon ..................... 89
Abimelech and Nightmares ..................... 90
Challenge ..................... 94

Chapter 5: Creating Something Real from Something Symbolic 95
Rational and Creative Thoughts ..................... 98
Dreams Reveal Unknown Thoughts ..................... 101
Inspiration for a Potter ..................... 103
"I Am the Bread" ..................... 104
A Scientific Dream ..................... 106
Nebuchadnezzar's Misunderstood Dream Image ..................... 106
Inspiration for Creating a Job ..................... 108

Chapter 6: God Is a God of Symbols ........................................ 111
God's Most Important Symbols ........................................ 114
Warning ........................................ 118
Water in dreams ........................................ 119
Symbols of Water from Scripture ........................................ 121
Some Suggested Symbols That Might Work For You ........................................ 123

Chapter 7: Telling Your Dreams ........................................ 131
The Benefits of Sharing Your Dreams ........................................ 132
Whom Do You Tell? ........................................ 136
What a Dream Partner Should and Shouldn't Say ........................................ 140
Telling Your Dreams In a Group ........................................ 143
Never Chase After a Dream Partner ........................................ 145
Beware of False Prophets ........................................ 146
Benefits Are Everlasting Riches ........................................ 151

Chapter 8: Famous Christians' Dreams ........................................ 153
St. Francis's Dream ........................................ 153
John Bosco's Dreams ........................................ 155
Ronald Reagan's Recurring Dream ........................................ 157
Warning Dream for Ronald Reagan ........................................ 157
Betty Robison's Dream ........................................ 158
John A. Sanford's Father's Dream ........................................ 159
Jarena Lee's Dream ........................................ 161
Rodney Howard-Browne's Dream ........................................ 163
Constantine's Dream ........................................ 164
Bill Johnson's Dream ........................................ 165
Kenneth E. Hagin's Dream ........................................ 166
Catherine Marshall's Dream ........................................ 168
A visitor's Dream with a Message for St. Augustine ........................................ 168
Pope John Paul II's Dream of the Homeless Cats ........................................ 169

Chapter 9: How the Dream Was Lost to the Church and How It Can Be Recovered ..... 175

Early Church Fathers Still Listening to God in Their Dreams ..... 178

The Dark Ages of Dreams ..... 180

From Aquinas and Freud ..... 182

Freud, Jung, and Exit of Dreams from the Church ..... 182

Two Important Witnesses in the Church—Kelsey and Sanford ..... 184

The Church's Call to Heal the Soul ..... 186

How the Church Can Draw Nearer to God with its Dreams . 189

Chapter 10: Drawing Nearer to God–Time to Take Action ..... 199

If You Are Afraid of God ..... 201

If You Feel Guilty ..... 205

If You Think You Are Unworthy ..... 206

Using Your Dreams to Get There ..... 207

Much Needed New Work of the Church ..... 209

The Role of the Spiritual Director in the Church ..... 210

Decision Time—What You Need to Do For Yourself ..... 213

What You Need to Do for Others ..... 216

A Personal Numinous Dream ..... 218

Charts ..... 221

Endnotes ..... 235

# Chapter 1: Understanding Your Dream's Language

> "As I began to take an interest in my dreams, I became aware for the first time in my life that God wanted to speak to me."
>
> Morton Kelsey, Author
> *Dreams: A Way to Listen to God*[1]

Dreams are so powerful—it only takes one to change your life forever. In the 1980s, I was searching for a way to draw nearer to God. I believed the scripture that said, "Draw near to God, and He will draw near to you" (James 4:8). My spiritual life needed a boost at that time, so I began searching for a Christian spiritual director, someone who would point the way for me. I soon found one and on the first visit she asked me, "What is God telling you in your dreams?" Sad to say, I didn't have a good answer. I had always been a prolific dreamer, and the fact that I didn't have an answer to her question was disappointing. I determined right then to start listening more closely to my dreams and to let them carry me where they would. Much to my surprise they carried me right into the arms of God.

Listening to my dreams became a part of who I am. My daily rituals include prayer, meditation, Bible reading, and journaling. Dream work remains a large part of my journal work. In the beginning I read every

Christian book on dreams I could find, which weren't very many. Soon people wanted to know what I was learning, and I was asked to speak to groups about Christian dream work. I attended workshops about dreaming and God. Eventually, people were coming to me for advice about their dreams. What began as a way for me to draw nearer to God flowed into my becoming a spiritual director with my own method of counseling other Christians about their relationships with God. My spiritual direction evolved through the years to include dream work, journaling, homework, Bible readings, and intimate conversations. Drawing nearer to God gave me a new life in Christ, a more intimate one. That life over time became a ministry. By being nearer to God I could hear His voice in my dreams, in my prayers, and in my reading of His word. My spiritual life became wholly integrated.

Very near the beginning of my ministry with dreams, I had the following dream. It gave me the comfort I needed to trust God fully with my life. With that newfound trust I could move forward with confidence in regard to listening to my dreams and obeying what God was telling me to do.

A twelve-story building stood before me. It contained no walls and looked like it was under construction. There was no roof.

From my view on the ground, I gazed up at the building. Then a voice spoke to me very clearly, and I knew that it was the voice of God. God said, "Go up to the top of the building and roll off."

I replied, "Okay." Even when awake, I am afraid of heights.

The climb up the ladder to the top of the building was long and arduous. When I reached the top floor, I walked over to the edge but didn't look down. I sat on the floor and then stretched out parallel to the edge. I crossed my arms over my chest and closed my eyes. Then I rolled to the left and fell out into open space.

I held my eyes tightly shut as I fell and fell and fell. Wind rushed past my ears. The fall seemed endless. The longer I fell, the more speed I gained, until I realized the ground must be close at hand.

Then all of a sudden I stopped in mid-air. I ventured to open my eyes and glanced below me. The ground was about three feet below me, and I was floating like a feather, light as can be, to the earth. I landed on my feet very softly.

When my feet touched ground, I yelled with all of my might, "Yes!" I threw my hands up to heaven and yelled again, "Yes!" I knew then by revelation that God had shown me how to trust Him without reservation and without fear.

## What Is a Dream?

Whether your dreams are action films or quiet, voice-only dreams, they are still dreams. And they mean something. They serve a purpose. You may think that unless God speaks to you in a revelation or you attend a dream workshop, you can never know what your dreams mean—not so. Understanding your dreams is easier than you may think. It simply takes practice, a little time, and some knowledge.

Generally, a dream is defined as a succession of spontaneous symbolic activities present in the mind during sleep, whether pictorial or auditory or both.

Dreams seem to gather information from our hearts, from our minds, and from our lives and present it back to us as a drama or a play with different parts of ourselves dressed up to look like someone we know.

Dreams serve a very important purpose to our spiritual lives, our psychological lives, and our physical lives, and that purpose is to heal us and make us whole. Therefore, they relentlessly endeavor to fulfill their purpose by presenting us with material with which to work in order to help us accomplish their purpose. Dreams walk into our lives when we're asleep and are helpless to keep them out. They talk to us and lead us to truths about ourselves that otherwise might take years in therapy to figure out. In one night it is possible to be healed of old hurts or to discover an answer to what we thought was an unanswerable question.

When we continuously avoid becoming whole, a dream will often pop to the surface of our conscious minds, presenting its message in symbolic language. It may even repeat and repeat until we grasp the message that something important is being conveyed.

Many of us are walking around daily, juggling to keep old resentments, hurts, and angers held under the surface of our conscious minds. When trying to understand dream material, think of yourself as holding those resentments and hurts like fifty Ping-Pong balls under water all at once. Just about the time you get five or six securely held under, a few get free and pop to the surface. You grab those that pop up. And the ones you were holding under water are now bobbing for your attention. Your efforts appear endless and energy-draining.

In your dream world, what pops up to the surface requires your attention. Therefore, the situation that needs healing will frequently *dress up* in the role of someone you know. And present itself to you in the form of a motion picture.

When you experience hurt feelings or a wounded spirit, sometimes you don't want to deal with the real problem. You may suppress your emotions or avoid dealing with the problem. Like the Ping-Pong balls, you hold your worries underneath the water of your unconscious mind daily. But when you sleep, you are helpless to keep the worries held down. And images from your unconscious are free to pop up to the surface, presenting you with solutions or messages that must get your attention.

One of the most common mistakes people make in trying to understand their dreams is they tend to believe their dream images are, in fact, the actual people they look like. Your dreams are primarily not about other people, but about you and your own soul. They are hardly ever about who they appear to be. The majority of your dreams are about you, your own problems, and your relationships with yourself, with your life, and with God.

Most dreams consist of images, much like a motion picture. Sometimes they appear in Technicolor, sometimes in black and white. Although most dreams look like action films, dreams can also be voice-only dreams with no pictures at all. Remember the dream that Solomon had in 1 Kings 3:5?

In that dream Solomon saw very little action. God simply appeared to Solomon and talked with him, offering Solomon a free gift. God said, "Ask what you wish me to give you." And Solomon answered, "… give thy servant an understanding heart to judge Thy people to discern between good and evil…" (1 Kings 3:9). Solomon obeyed God by relating the desire of his heart. And God reciprocated with a gift—wisdom—freely given.

When the young girl, Mary, became pregnant with Jesus, and Joseph, her betrothed, contemplated putting her away quietly, an angel appeared to Joseph in a dream and spoke with him saying, "Joseph, son of David, do not be afraid to take Mary as your wife; for that which has been conceived in her is of the Holy Spirit. And she will bear a Son; and you shall call His name Jesus, for it is He who will save His people from their sins" (Matthew 1:20-21).

In that dream there is no action, but only an angel telling forth. This "no-action" type dream happens not only in the Bible, but also happens to ordinary people like you and me. However, the most common type of dream is the action-packed drama dream. Frequently these action dreams have characters who chase you or hold you hostage. After a night of dreaming about foreign spies or dark menacing characters, you may sit up in bed the next morning and ask in frustration, "Who *are* these people?" The truth of the matter is: they are *you*—all of them. They are not the people they appear to be, but are, in fact, representatives of different aspects of your personality. And they've come to help you, to reveal yourself to you, and to heal you.

Whether your dream is an action-packed thriller, a voice with no picture, or something in between, if God wants to speak with you, He will find a way. And if you are too busy during the day to spend time with God, God will sometimes *intrude* when you are most unable to turn yourself off to Him—while you are sleeping. If you have a dream in which God speaks to you, you will know it. And you will remember it. Most likely, you will never be the same.

## How Often Do You Dream?

"The most number of dreams I remember having in one night is four," revealed Sharon, an active dreamer. Sharon was flipping through her dream journal pointing out various dreams labeled *Dream 1, Dream 2* and so forth all having occurred in succession during one night.

Sleep researchers say that on a typical night a person may dream from five to seven times. However, I have found it to be unusual that anyone remembers more than three or four dreams in one night. Each dream usually lasts from fifteen to ninety minutes. The dreams which occur nearest to waking are the ones that are easiest to remember.[2]

There are generally four phases of sleeping. Phase 1) The level which I call *limbo* is the period of time when you first feel drowsy, between being wide awake and sound asleep—when you are totally relaxed and feel as if you are asleep—but actually aren't. You can still hear sounds in the house and can be alert in a flash. Phase 2) This phase is deeper than *limbo* and leads to a sounder sleep. Phase 3) This is the deepest phase of sleep. Phase 4) The last phase of sleep before awakening, where dreams are most easily remembered. This is the phase in which REM (rapid eye movement) takes place and most dreaming occurs. It is fairly close to the surface of your sleep period. A person can experience this dream sequence several times during a night.[3]

## Holding Onto Your Dreams

Has this ever happened to you? The alarm clock buzzer jars you awake and about the time you reach over to kill it with a slap, you hear the baby crying from an adjoining bedroom. So you grab your robe and hit the floor running. Sadly, all the dreams you had during the night fly right out the window.

Or maybe the clock radio awakens you to the 7:00 a.m. drive-time disc jockey or the highway helicopter announcer describing the back up at the intersection of Such-'n-Such and So-'n-So Roads. Somewhere in the back of your mind the name of the street registers as being on your route to work. You grab the radio knob and twist it up to loud. And your dream is long gone.

Can God get through to you in your hectic schedule? Do you make time for God in your daily routine?

You might say, "I'll spend thirty minutes with God today." But when? During the commute to work? Does He get your *undivided* attention in the car? Or after you put your children to bed at night and you are tired?

With your particular habits, how many dreams can you remember nightly? One? Two? Some people remember two or three dreams a night. Others only remember one. Many people have told me they never dream. It is very frustrating not to remember any dreams. Fully intending to remember their dreams, they've tried placing a pad of paper on the night stand before retiring. But as soon as the buzz of the alarm clock goes off, their dream slate is wiped clean.

First of all, it is important to understand: Remembering your dreams is a habit—a habit which takes practice to establish, much like playing the piano or riding a bicycle. So, first of all, commit to remembering your dreams, and then practice, practice, practice. Tell yourself nightly, "Tonight I will remember my dreams." And keep telling yourself every night for at least thirty nights in a row.

After thirty nights of practice you should be remembering at least one dream a night. Of course, if you also commit to recording your dreams, you'll probably start remembering multiple dreams per night. It seems that when you begin to take your dreams seriously, your unconscious begins to take your commitment seriously, and it begins to feed your conscious mind more and more dream material to work with, resembling a snowball effect.

One of the exercises I teach in my dream workshops is to give yourself permission to remember your dreams. Often we don't remember our dreams because we unconsciously don't want to remember them. Therefore, if before falling asleep you say aloud to yourself, "Tonight I give myself permission to remember any and all dreams that I may have," oftentimes, just doing that simple exercise will bring down any walls you've erected to keep out disturbing dreams. Then all dreams can flow into your conscious mind.

If you try those two exercises—practicing remembering your dreams and giving yourself permission to remember—and you still don't remember your dreams, try prayer. Repent if you have ever said that you wouldn't remember your dreams. Ask God to remove any walls or hindrances that you might have placed between your unconscious and conscious minds. Then trust that He will answer your prayer. Put your faith to work on your dream life. Then relax and give it time.

There are several reasons why we don't remember our dreams. Listed below are a few of those reasons:

- We don't really want to remember them!
- Fear of nightmares.
- Waking up to too much noise, such as alarm clocks, yelling children, or television.
- Severe illness, which affects dream patterns.
- We don't believe that dreams are important.

If you have intentionally blocked your dream life, you will remember very few dreams, if any. In one workshop, an elderly woman raised her hand to ask a question, concluding with, "I don't remember any dreams, but I don't want to. My dreams are always bad, and I don't want to know what they say."

If remembering dreams is a problem for you, maybe the fear of having nightmares has affected your ability to remember. Maybe fear has temporarily *clogged* the flow of dream material from your unconscious to your conscious mind. Unclog the flow by giving yourself permission to remember—even if you have another nightmare that frightens you. Muster your courage to stand strong and be healed. Nightmares are only trying to get your attention. When you begin paying attention to the characters in your dreams, nightmares will cease.

If you truly desire to remember your dreams, try to eliminate every possible hindrance to dream recall. That might mean asking your husband or wife not to wake you up in the morning by talking to you. It might mean closing the door to your bedroom, so the children won't come bouncing into your bed at the crack of dawn. It also might mean buying a different alarm clock, one with a *quiet* buzzer.

In a perfect world of dream recall, dreamers would wake up when their body's own inner alarm clock wakes them up. They would have five or ten minutes of quiet to savor their dreams and to replay them in their minds. Then they would reach for their notepad on the night stand and jot down their dreams in detail.

Mary Jackson experienced a period in her life when she was seriously ill with neurological problems. The symptoms had affected her brainwave patterns, which affected her dream life. Sometimes she would not remember dreams at all. Other times she would know she dreamed, but the dream would be just out of reach. Mary also took prescribed medications, which could have affected her dream patterns.

At a dream workshop Mary wanted to know, "If the medications are affecting my dreams, do I still write them down?"

"Yes," I recommended. "If you have acquired the habit of remembering your dreams and have been recording them, don't break the habit. Keep practicing remembering. You can decide later whether you want to interpret those dreams or not, but don't break a habit that is beneficial or one you'll have to re-establish later."

If you want to remember your dreams, here are eight tips that will help:

1. When you first awake, replay your dream over in your mind before you first open your eyes.

2. Write your dream down and keep it in a notebook or journal.

3. Draw your dreams.

4. Interpret your dreams.

5. Write a dialogue with dream figures.

6. Research symbols from your dreams in the Bible.

7. Tell your dreams to a trusted friend.
8. Pray and ask God to help you remember your dreams.

If you believe your dreams are not important, you probably won't write them down. You probably won't pay much attention to them at all. You may or may not be able to recall them. The problem is not that you might miss out on some interesting dreams, but that you might be closing off another avenue through which you can draw nearer to God.

Remember Joseph, Mary's husband, and ask yourself, "What if Joseph hadn't listened to his dream when an angel spoke to him and told him to get up and take Mary and the baby to Egypt because Herod was going to kill the babies?" What if…

## Tell Me What They Look Like

A Caucasian woman related the following dream to me:

> I was in a cafeteria, and there were only African-American men there with me. They were Christians, and I knew them, and they were my friends. We were all laughing and talking and having a good time. It looked like a school cafeteria with long cafeteria tables. We were talking about the Lord. I loved these men, and they loved me. I felt very warm and close to them. I loved their spirits.

Dreams, very often, look familiar. The scenery of our dreams is often our homes, our jobs, our schools, or our churches. And very often they look like full-length Technicolor movies. At other times, a dream may be a short feature with only a word or two with no picture, or a picture with no words. Dream figures can look like people we know or complete strangers. Like us or different from us, people in our dreams often seem familiar.

Frequently those dreams that are in color seem so real that when you wake up, you aren't sure you were dreaming. However, there are exceptions to what we would think of as *normal* dreams. Dreamers have reported dreams in which they speak foreign languages they don't know when awake, or they fly in their dreams without airplanes, or water flows uphill, or inanimate objects communicate with them. Even animals can talk with us in our dreams.

Dreams don't always act in what we would call a *normal* way. The reason is that the language of dreams is a symbolic language, and it must be viewed symbolically and spiritually. Understanding your dreams requires that you shift your thinking a little—like learning a new language.

Morton Kelsey, the author of *God, Dreams and Revelation*, writes, "When men forget how to think symbolically, the symbols of dreams become a closed book."[4] Thinking symbolically requires a shift in our thinking. We can no longer see a tree and think of it only as a tree. We must ask ourselves, "What does a tree mean to me *symbolically*?"

In a dream if a tree reaches out and embraces you, it means something—something different from a tree merely hugging you. Maybe it means what the book of Revelation says, "...the leaves of the tree were for the healing of the nations" (Revelation 22:2).

If you dream a sexy dream about a coworker, don't assume that you have deep-seated desires for that person. First remember that the characters in your dreams are generally not the people they appear to be, but rather are parts of your own personality that have dressed themselves up as someone you know and come to visit you in your dreams. They've come with a purpose, to bring about your healing.

So when you dream about a coworker or your boss or your neighbor, remember that that character is part of you. Ask yourself, "What is there about my boss that is like me? Do I act like that sometimes? What is he trying to tell me? Or do I have any personality traits that are similar to my neighbor's? Do I gossip like her? Do I admire me? Do I want to learn to love myself?"

If you still don't understand what the character means, try having a dialogue with it. Write on a piece of paper, the name of the character, and then beside the name, write what you think the character is saying to you. On the next line write your own name, then what you would answer back. Continue your conversation on paper, until you understand what the character means. Most of the time, understanding comes quickly.

To interpret the symbols in your dream, take a clean sheet of paper and write the symbol in the center of the page, draw a circle around it. Then write what that symbol means to you nearby and draw a circle around that. Next, draw a line connecting the first word to the second. It is possible to have several associations with the first symbol. Create an association sheet for each of the symbols in your dream.

Sample Association Sheet:

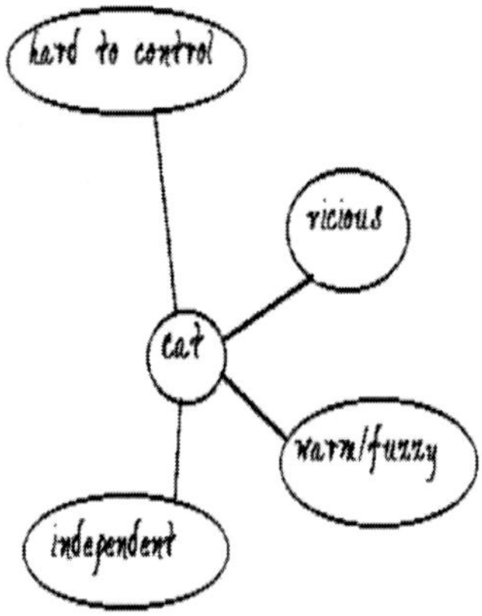


Then go back and reread the dream. In light of your associations, the meanings of the symbols will soon become clear. If they don't, try researching the symbol in the Bible. Look up the word in a concordance and see what God's Word says on the subject. If you have Bible software on your computer, do some research electronically. Also, pray about the symbol. Ask God what it means.

Keith Clark, former vicar provincial for the Midwest Province of the Capuchin Friars and author of *Make Space, Make Symbols* writes:

> ...The symbols we use to open the door for Him to come in to us as we are, are as important for us as the meeting tent was for the Israelites... even though the Israelites were a people who were sometimes wandering, sometimes on a journey to a definite destination, they always carried with them the meeting tent. Every time they pitched camp, they set up the meeting tent. There Moses and the elders entered into God's presence to receive direction and instruction for the Israelite community."[5]

Very much like the Israelites, as we travel on our own inner journey, our symbols should always be kept in our minds and on our hearts. As Clark says, "Always in their midst was the meeting tent. But it was the symbol of what and who they were, a people chosen and led by God. Our own personal symbols, as well as those of our religious tradition, are like the meeting tent which the Israelites set up each time they made their camp."[6]

Faithfulness to our personal dream symbols on our inner journey simply reminds us of who we are in Christ. And not only who we are, but *whose* we are. Morton Kelsey points out that "...if...images are given quiet, meditative attention, they can be...persuaded to speak of meanings from all levels of being. ...one begins to discover that the ways of communicating with the Risen Christ are just as natural and actually not very different from making contact with an inner dream figure."[7]

You may be thinking, "I've never talked with an inner dream figure."

That may be true, but it can be done. The difference is practice; faithfulness to practice dream work; and quiet, meditative attention to what your dreams have to tell you.

When the true meaning of your dream becomes clear to you, you will know it. You will have an *aha* reaction at first. Then you will have peace. And you'll say something like, "Oh, that's what that means!" or, "Hey, that's it! That makes perfect sense."

Sometimes it takes many tries to interpret a dream, sometimes even years. No matter how long it takes, it is worth the effort to know what God is trying to tell you. You've heard the saying, "A picture is worth a thousand words." It is true. Pictures in our minds in the night can say infinitely more than words. If our dreams were in words to be read, they'd be very dull indeed. As it is, the symbols in our sleep speak personal messages especially designed for our own understanding.

After you have been writing your dreams down for a few months or a year, you'll begin to see repeating symbols, such as numbers, inanimate objects, people, and places. It is a good idea to tape a piece of paper inside the front cover of your dream journal (see chapter 3), and to keep a record of these personal dream symbols and what they mean to you. Soon you'll be able to recognize instantly in your dreams what those symbols mean. They will have become a sort of alphabet in your own dream language.

## What Do Dreams Sound Like?

Dreams sound very normal and natural to the dreamer. Horns honk, voices yell, and bells ring. Dream sounds don't seem to be as noticeable as dream visuals, however. Dreamers hardly ever mention sounds when relating a dream. This tells me that sounds in a dream must not be out of the ordinary.

## What If You Don't Dream?

If you are one of those people who doesn't remember ever having had a single dream, you are not alone. Many people think they never dream. However, scientific studies have shown that every person dreams, even if they don't remember their dreams. Every person dreams every night.

It has been proven in sleep laboratories that dreaming is essential to our physical and mental health. In the 1950s there was a young doctor in Chicago, William Dement, who was testing sleepers in various ways. He discovered that deprivation of dreams seriously disturbed sleepers and had important implications for mental health.[8]

The basic factor that seems to determine whether people remember their dreams or not is their degree of interest. If you continually ignore your dreams, your ability to remember becomes more and more diminished, until you really can't remember. The real danger is not in encouraging dreams to come to you, but in blocking them out of your life.

Reading about dreams is both fun and interesting. It seems that everyone is curious about other people's dreams and their own. However, the real work begins when you make the decision to actually do dream work and to really know yourself and God.

When I speak to a group about dreams, I find that almost everyone is curious about dreams. It's easy to get excited about the possibilities of having a real experience with the Lord. We all want to "taste and see that the Lord is good" (Psalm 34:8). Working with dreams is an interior adventure, and it takes a certain amount of self-discipline. But anyone armed with a pen and paper and a desire to go deeper can do dream work.

Always remember this: God wants a relationship with you. He wants someone to talk with. One night in your sleep when you least expect it, He may knock at your door and say, "I stand at the door and knock; if anyone hears My voice and opens the door, I will come in to him, and will dine with him, and he with Me" (Revelation 3:20). I know because He's done that to me.

So, besides simply being curious about dreams, which is good, I want to encourage you to seriously listen to your dreams and give them consideration. Understanding your dreams, yourself, and God naturally draws you nearer to Him.

## What is the Purpose of Dreams?

In *Dreams: A Way to Listen to God*, Morton Kelsey says, "I have discovered that the dream attempts to show us how to develop toward wholeness."[9] It seems that just as our bodies continually strive toward good health by healing themselves over and over again, our soul also continually strives toward wholeness and perfection through dreaming.

According to Kelsey, "Jesus introduced (the idea)… that the Kingdom of God is within us and among us."[10] It seems that when God created humanity He implanted an image within each one of us that is His image of our highest selves. Without our realizing it, dreams, as the impetus for this growth, feed us seed, in the form of symbols and messages that hopefully, gradually creates the very image God desires for each one of us, thus bringing about His purpose.

Mark 4:26 shows us that this theory seems very plausible, because Jesus says, "The Kingdom of God is like a man who casts seed upon the soil; and goes to bed at night and gets up by day, and the seed sprouts up and grows—how, he himself does not know. The soil produces crops *by itself*; first the blade, then the head, then the mature grain in the head." In other words, a perfect crop is made in His image.

It could be said that God is the *seed caster*, casting continual seed upon the soil of our souls, and every night the seed grows in our dreams, healing our souls and recreating us into His perfect image.

# Chapter 2: Knowing Your Dream Type

> To these four young men God gave knowledge and understanding of all kinds of literature and learning. And Daniel could understand visions and dreams of all kinds.
>
> Daniel 1:17 NIV

Have you ever awakened in the morning with a dream fresh on your mind and wondered, "What was that?" You walk around all day with the feeling that God is trying to tell you something. You ask yourself, "Was God trying to teach me something? Was He warning me about an event before it happens? What kind of dream was that, anyway?"

It might be a surprise to you, but just as Daniel could understand dreams of all kinds, so can you. When you know what type of dream you've dreamed, you can use that knowledge to better understand the meaning of it. When you understand the meaning of your dream, you will draw nearer to God simply because you'll realize that two-way communication is taking place between you and the Lord Most High.

Learning to recognize all kinds of dreams is not as difficult as it may seem at first. The chart in the back of the book entitled *Dreams in the Bible* makes a helpful tool to recognize the types of dreams located in the

Bible. Over the past thirty years of working with my dreams, I've discovered many types of dreams—following are fifteen types, along with an example dream for each.

## A Promise Dream

Has God ever made you a promise? Yes, He has. He has made you a lot of promises in His Word, such as, "I will never leave you nor forsake you" (Hebrews 13:5 NKJV). But has He ever made you a promise in a dream? He did do that for Jacob. Jacob, who was later renamed Israel, had a dream at Bethel (Genesis 28:12). He dreamed he saw a ladder with the angels of God ascending and descending on it. In the dream, God made certain promises to Jacob. See if you can find all of God's promises to Jacob in his dream.

> And he had a dream, and behold, a ladder was set on the earth with its top reaching to heaven; and behold, the angels of God were ascending and descending on it. And behold, the Lord stood above it and said, 'I am the Lord, the God of your father Abraham and the God of Isaac; the land on which you lie, I will give it to you and to your descendants. Your descendants shall also be like the dust of the earth, and you shall spread out to the west and to the east and to the north and to the south; and in you and in your descendants shall all the families of the earth be blessed. And behold, I am with you and will keep you wherever you go, and will

> bring you back to this land; for I will not leave you until I have done what I have promised you.
>
> Genesis 28:12-15

If you found seven promises, you are correct. 1) God promised the land, 2) God promised many descendants, 3) God promised that Jacob's descendants would cover a large area, 4) God promised that all the families of the earth would be blessed, 5) God promised that He was with Jacob, 6) God promised to be with Jacob wherever he went, and 7) God promised that He would bring Jacob back to that land.

Interestingly, this dream was so powerful with promises that Jacob couldn't keep from taking some action, even though he was afraid he recognized that something special was happening to him. He anointed the stone he was sleeping on and gave it a name, "Bethel." Then he made a promise back to God that if he would be kept safe on his journey, then the Lord would be his God. He vowed to God that the place where the stone was would be God's house and that he would give back to God one-tenth of whatever God gave to him. This promise dream changed Jacob's life forever.

## A Warning Dream

Perhaps the most famous warning dream of our time is the dream that Abraham Lincoln told to his wife shortly before his assassination in 1865. This is his warning dream:

About ten days ago I retired very late. I had been up waiting for important dispatches from the front. I could not have been long in bed when I fell into a slumber, and I was weary. I soon began to dream. There seemed to be a death-like stillness about me. Then I heard subdued sobs, as if a number of people were weeping. I thought I left my bed and wandered downstairs. There the silence was broken by the same pitiful sobbing, but the mourners were invisible. I went from room to room; no living person was in sight, but the same mournful sounds of distress met me as I passed along. I saw light in all the rooms, every object was familiar to me; but where were all the people who were grieving as if their hearts would break? I was puzzled and alarmed. What could be the meaning of all this? Determined to find the cause of a state of things so mysterious and so shocking, I kept on until I arrived at the East Room, which I entered. There I met with a sickening surprise. Before me was a catafalque on which rested a corpse wrapped in funeral vestments. Around it were stationed soldiers who were acting as guards; and there was a throng of people, gazing mournfully upon the corpse, whose face was covered, others weeping pitifully. 'Who is dead in the White House?' I demanded of one of the soldiers. 'The President' was his answer, 'he was killed by an assassin.' Then came a loud burst of grief from the crowd, which woke me from my dream. I slept no more that night; and although it was only a dream, I have been strangely annoyed by it ever since.[11]

Warning dreams are an exception to the *rule* that says everyone in the dream is part of you. Unlike other dreams, warnings are about whom they seem to be about and are a call to action. By their nature they come *before* an event. Wise and experienced dreamers heed warning dreams and call their prayer warriors to begin the battle on their behalf. If Lincoln had only known that his dream was a warning dream, he might have drawn nearer to God for his safety and protection and avoided the assassin's bullet.

## A Blessing Dream

God is so good and He loves us so much. Like our parents, sometimes He wants to bless us by giving us gifts. Such was the dream of Solomon in 1 Kings 3:5-14. It tells of Solomon's blessing dream. The scripture says, "In Gibeon the Lord appeared to Solomon in a dream at night, and God said, 'Ask what you wish me to give you.'"

Verses 9-12 give Solomon's response in the dream:

> So give Thy servant an understanding heart to judge Thy people, to discern between good and evil. And it was pleasing in the sight of the Lord that Solomon had asked this thing. And God said to him, "Because you have asked this thing and have not asked for yourself long life, nor have you asked riches for yourself, nor have you asked for the life of your enemies, but have asked for yourself discernment to understand justice, behold, I have done according to your words."
>
> 1 Kings 3:9-12

Like Jacob, Solomon awoke and was compelled to show his gratitude to God for the dream. He went immediately to Jerusalem to stand in the presence of God before the Ark of the Covenant where he offered burnt offerings and made peace offerings. Then to further show his gratitude he made a feast for his servants (1 Kings 3:15). Solomon's actions prove how important one single dream can be to our lives.

## Numinous Dreams

According to Merriam Webster's Collegiate Dictionary, numinous means *filled with a sense of the presence of divinity.*[12] Dreams of angels, of seeing or being with Jesus, or of seeing or being in heaven are all considered numinous dreams. Jacob's dream (Genesis 28:12-15), in which he saw a ladder reaching up into heaven with angels ascending and descending on it, definitely qualifies as a numinous dream. So does Joseph's dream about the angel instructing him to marry Mary (Matthew 1:20). Joseph's dream about the angel telling him to flee to Egypt is also a numinous dream (Matthew 2:13-14). Also, the dream about the angel telling him in Egypt to pack up and return to Israel qualifies as a numinous dream (Matthew 2:19-23).

Dreams that are filled with the presence of divinity hold a great deal of power. If you ever experience a numinous dream, chances are you will never forget it. When the Rev. A. J. Gordon, the renowned Baptist preacher and author from Boston, told of a numinous dream he had, he said it changed the course of his ministry.

He dreamed that he was preaching one day when a stranger entered his church and slowly made his way up the aisle. The man attended the whole service but left quickly after it was over. Gordon asked someone in the church who the stranger was, and the answer was, "Why, do you not know that man? It was Jesus of Nazareth."

When Gordon realized that he had not recognized Christ, a rush of emotion filled him. He began asking himself life-changing questions about his ministry that he would have never thought to ask without the dream. As a result, A. J. Gordon was never the same after his dream.[13] After experiencing numinous dreams, people have written plays, symphonies, and books. Some have invented musical instruments, medicines, and great works of art. Such art forms have a sense of the holy about them simply because they are replicas of the divine.

## A Prophetic Dream

Prophetic dreams are those that *foretell* events. Such dreams tell of things to come, much like what the apostle John wrote about in John 16:13, concerning the function of the Holy Spirit, "…and He will disclose to you what is to come." Dreams that foretell coming events cause us to ask questions, such as, "How would the world be different if someone had paid attention to their prophetic dreams?"

In early March 1981 an English housewife named Barbara Garwell dreamed that she was riding in a car with two Germans who wore uniforms resembling those of the Nazi SS. In the dream a large limousine approached and stopped, and a man stepped out whom Garwell uncertainly identified as a well-known actor. The two SS men got out of their car; one drew a pistol and fired several shots at the actor, who fell to the ground.

Three weeks later, on March 30, 1981, the former actor and then-president, Ronald Reagan, stepped out of his limousine and was shot and severely wounded by John Hinckley, Jr. Hinckley had once been a member of a neo-Nazi group, but was expelled in 1978 because of his violent ideas.[14] Perhaps she could have called the Secret Service and reported it. Would anyone have believed her dream? I don't know. But I do believe God was trying to warn someone.

## A Teaching Dream

The Word of the Lord came to Jeremiah, the prophet, and said in Jeremiah 33:3, "Call to Me, and I will answer you, and I will tell you great and mighty things, which you do not know." How will God tell us these awesome things that we do not know? In times of prayer or meditation? Through sermons or worship? Or could they be revealed through our dreams?

Joseph Shabalala, a black South African minister and founder/lead singer of Ladysmith Black Mambazo, believes that God teaches him things he does not know in his dreams. As a result of his teaching dreams, he has recorded twenty-five albums and created two tracks on Paul Simon's *Graceland* album. Anyone who has heard Ladysmith's songs realizes that their music is uniquely soulful and spiritual. An issue of *Time* magazine reported Joseph's dream that inspired his music:

> Every time when I am sleeping, I have music in my mind. All the time, like when you sleep, like a dream. There is a stage, but there are children not on stage. They are between the stage and the sky, floating and always singing. They are like my teachers who teach me exactly this sound.[15]

## A Comforting Dream

God loves us so much that He has compassion for us in times of trouble, mourning, or afflictions. When hard times come, God pours out His comfort in order to bring understanding and relief. The apostle Paul wrote to the Corinthians, telling them of this comfort. In 2 Corinthians 1:3, he wrote, "Blessed be the God and Father of our Lord Jesus Christ, the Father of mercies and God of *all* comfort..." Therefore, if we are comforted in our dreams, that comfort must come from God. It is His comfort sent to heal us.

In *Dreams: God's Forgotten Language*, John A. Sanford tells about a middle-aged woman whom he knew who experienced a comforting dream two years after her four-month-old baby died.

> In my dream I saw a young woman of about thirty grasping the hand of a small boy, just learning to walk. I knew instantly that the boy was ours...I noticed his sturdy little legs particularly. They were running freely and hap-

> pily up a gentle slope.... I thought that (the young woman) was someone very near to me. I awakened my husband to tell him of my dream because it was so vivid, and I got such great comfort from it. I said, "I believe that was my grandmother with our baby, because I felt so close to her and he is all right because she is taking care of him." I felt very happy...[16]

## A Healing Dream

Some people have reported dreams where the dreamer is directed to change dietary habits or behavior patterns in order to enjoy better health. Others have discussed dreams in which they are spontaneously healed, with symptoms never returning.

The author Janice Baylis described an experience of great pain in her right eye. She made an appointment for an eye examination, but the day before the exam, she took an afternoon nap and had the following dream:

> I am looking at a bubble of water on our patio. A fish is swimming in it... The bubble changes to a spotted light with a dark center. It begins to move toward me. I am very glad that I am going to be immersed in that light. As the light reaches me I feel a tingling, electrified sensation strongly centered in my right eye.

When Janice awoke, the pain in her right eye was gone, and it checked out fine in the exam the following day.[17]

## Two Helping Dreams

Sometimes a helping dream helps more than one person. When the Pharaoh in Egypt dreamed two helping dreams in one night, and Joseph interpreted the dreams, not only was the nation of Egypt helped, but so was Joseph.

The Pharaoh dreamed that he was standing by the Nile, and:

> …lo, from the Nile there came up seven cows, sleek and fat; and they grazed in the marsh grass. Then behold, seven other cows, came up after them from the Nile, ugly and gaunt, and they stood by the other cows on the bank of the Nile. And the ugly and gaunt cows ate up the seven sleek and fat cows (Genesis 41:1-4).

Then Pharaoh awoke. And he fell asleep and dreamed a second time:

> …behold, seven ears of grain came up on a single stalk, plump and good. Then behold, seven ears, thin and scorched by the east wind, sprouted up after them. And the thin ears swallowed up the seven plump and full ears (Genesis 41:5-7).

Then Pharaoh awoke, and behold, it was a dream.

After Pharaoh sought an interpretation from his wise men and received no plausible answer, he sent for Joseph (Genesis 41:14). The two dreams had one meaning. Seven years of great abundance were coming to Egypt followed by seven years of a severe famine.

Joseph's advice to Pharaoh was that he locate a wise and discerning man and put him in charge of Egypt. His advice included setting aside a fifth of the produce of the land in the years of abundance, so there would be sufficient supply in the years of lack (Genesis 41:33).

As a result of Joseph's wise counsel to Pharaoh, he was put in charge over all the land of Egypt, and when the seven years of famine came "over all the face of the earth, then Joseph opened all the store houses and sold to the Egyptians…and the people of all the earth came to Egypt to buy grain from Joseph" (Genesis 41:37-57).

Not only were Pharaoh and Joseph helped as a result of the helping dreams, but so were countless other people.

## A Correcting Dream

Proverbs 3:11-12, says, "My son, do not reject the discipline of the Lord, or loathe His reproof. For whom the Lord loves He reproves, even as a father, the son in whom He delights." Jerome was a man well acquainted with God's reproof—which came to him in the form of a dream.

Jerome lived from AD 345 to 420 and is best known for having translated the Bible into the common language of the people. His translation is known as the Vulgate. Evidently Jerome loved to read the Bible, but he also read and collected the writings of many pagan writers, including Cicero and other prominent philosophers.

In Jerome's dream, he was dragged before the judgment seat, which was surrounded by light. He was asked who and what he was, "I replied: 'I am a Christian.' But He who presided said: 'Thou liest, thou are a follower of Cicero and not of Christ. For where thy treasure is, there will thy heart be also." He was ordered to be scourged and received many lashes. But he admitted, "I was tortured more severely still by the fire of conscience."

Jerome cried out for mercy in the dream and some bystanders fell on their knees and pleaded with the Judge to allow Jerome a chance to repent. Jerome swore an oath saying, "Lord, if ever again I possess worldly books, or if ever again I read such, I have denied Thee."

When Jerome awakened, his eyes were drenched with tears and his shoulders were black and blue. He resolved thereafter saying, "...I felt the bruises long after I awoke from my sleep, and that thenceforth I read the books of God with a zeal greater than I had previously given to the books of men." [18]

## An Encouraging Dream

Monica, the Christian mother of Augustine, prayed many years for her son. Because he was an intelligent and gifted child, his parents sent him from his home in Tagaste in Numidia to Carthage to study. There he took a mistress and before his eighteenth birthday she gave birth to a son, Adeodatus. In Carthage, Augustine began to study the writings of Cicero and other philosophers and eventually joined a sect known as the Manichaeans. Still, his mother prayed.

Then she had a dream that gave her encouragement and hope. In her dream Monica was standing on a ruler (a rule of faith). An angel approached her and asked why she was sorrowful. Monica answered that it was the perdition of her son that she was lamenting. The angel assured her that where she was, there also would her son be (also standing on a rule of faith).

Later, Augustine moved to Milan and became friends with St. Ambrose. He began to zealously study the Bible and was baptized by St. Ambrose, along with his son, Adeodatus. Before leaving Italy for Africa, Augustine wrote treatises against the Manichaeans. Three years later he was ordained a priest and served thirty-five years as the Bishop of Hippo. Augustine's most famous writings include *The Confessions*, *The City of God*, and *On Christian Doctrine*.

Monica's dream encouraged her concerning the future of her son, but it also encouraged Augustine, who said to God in prayer, "Thou sendest Thine hand from above, and drewest my soul out of that profound darkness, when my mother, Thy faithful one, wept to Thee on my behalf more than mothers are wont to weep over the bodily deaths of their children. For she saw that I was dead by that faith and spirit which she had from Thee, and Thou heardest her, O Lord."[19]

## A Problem-solving Dream

Elias Howe, inventor of the sewing machine, was working unsuccessfully to perfect the lock-stitch method of sewing. He had been using a needle shank that had a hole in the middle of the shank, but then he had a nightmare that turned out to be a blessing.

In the dream he was surrounded by cannibals and sitting in a pot about to be boiled. Suddenly he noticed that the natives were wielding spears, which had eye-shaped holes near their tips. Upon waking from the dream, he whittled a model of the spear and discovered the *solution* to his sewing machine problem.[20]

## A Directing Dream

During a time when Alexander the Great and his armies were moving through all of Asia, conquering cities such as Damascus, Sidon, and Tyre, Alexander sent a letter to Juddua, the high priest of the Jews. He asked him for supplies for his army. In return he promised presents—presents just like the ones he had sent to Darius, king of the Persians.

Juddua answered the letter saying that he had given his oath to Darius that he would not bear arms against him as long as he was living. Upon hearing this, Alexander was furious and vowed to make an expedition against the Jewish high priest.

After Alexander's seige of Tyre, he set out for Jerusalem, laying siege to Gaza along the way. When Jaddua, the high priest, heard about Alexander's anger and revenge plans, he was in agony. In his desperation he ordered all the people to pray to God and to join him in offering sacrifices to God. He drew near to God and sought protection for the nation, depending on God to deliver them from their enemies. Then he had a dream.

God *directed* Juddua in his dream to take courage, to adorn the city, and to open the city gates. All the people should dress in white garments, except for him and the priests who should meet Alexander *in the habits proper to their order* without the dread of any ill consequences, which the providence of God would prevent.[21]

When Juddua woke from his dream, he greatly rejoiced. His response was to do everything he had been directed to do by the dream. Then he waited.

Timing was everything, and when Juddua heard that Alexander was not far from the city, he and all the citizens processed out.

Alexander could see the procession marching out from a long distance away in their white garments and with the priests in their purple robes. He saw the high priest with his high miter on his head and wearing the gold plate, which had the name of God engraved across the front. Alexander was in awe! He separated himself from his army and rode alone, slowly, toward the Jewish high priest adoring the name he saw written in gold!

As Alexander approached Juddua, he saluted him. And the Jews, in one voice, saluted Alexander. And all gathered around him. The Syrian kings who stood watching this event could hardly believe it. They thought Alexander had lost his mind.

But one brave king approached Alexander and asked, "How is it that when all others adore you, that you adore the high priest of the Jews?"

And Alexander replied.

> I did not adore him, but that God who hath honoured him with his high priesthood; for I saw this very person in a dream, in this very habit, when I was at Dios in Macedonia, who, when I was considering with myself how I might obtain the dominion of Asia, exhorted

> me to make no delay, but boldly to pass over the sea thither, for that he would conduct my army, and would give me the dominion over the Persians; when it is, that having seen no other in that habit, and now seeing this person in it, and remembering that vision, and the exhortation which I had in my dream, I believe that I bring this army, under the divine conduct…

Then Alexander and Juddua shook hands and went into the city, with the other priests running along side. Once inside the city, Alexander went to the temple and offered a sacrifice to God, according to the high priest's directions. When the book of Daniel was opened and read where it said that the Greeks should destroy the empire of the Persians, Alexander supposed that he was that person.

The next day he called all the citizens of the city together and asked them what favors they wanted, and the high priest answered that they wanted to continue to live according to the laws of their forefathers and that they might pay no taxes in the seventh year. And Alexander granted their desires.

He asked if any of the men would like to join his army, assuring them that they could live according to the laws of their forefathers. Many were ready to join. When Alexander had settled these issues in Jerusalem, he left with his army, moving into neighboring cities.[22]

Jerusalem was left in peace, because Juddua, the high priest, had depended on God to deliver him and all the people from war. Then he responded to the directions given in his dream.

## Giving of a Ministry Dream

In the year AD 303 there was a young man named Nicholas who was imprisoned during the reign of Emperor Diocletian, when many Christians were persecuted. However, he was freed when Constantine became a Christian and allowed religious freedom for all. In the city of Myra, the chief city of his province, the bishop died, and members of the council tried unsuccessfully to elect a successor. Then the oldest official had a dream.

In his dream the official was told to stand at the cathedral door the next day and to choose the first man named Nicholas who came through the door as the new bishop. When Nicholas arrived at church for morning prayer, he was asked his name, and soon afterward was elected by the council as bishop.

At one point in his career, Nicholas had the opportunity to visit the Holy Land. His visit had such a dramatic impact on him, he decided to resign as bishop and stay where Christ had lived. But God commanded him in a dream to return to Myra, so he obeyed the Lord.

Nicholas was a very popular Bishop and was loved because of his generosity. It was said that he often disguised himself and distributed gifts to children. Through the years there were many stories passed down about Nicholas and his Christlike spirit. And after his death he was named the patron saint of Russia and of youth. It is from this true saint that we have seen the myth of Saint Nicholas (Santa Claus) develop.[23]

# A Turning Point Dream

For some people a dream can be a turning point in their lives. Seemingly, one day their lives are headed in one direction, and after a certain dream, they turn completely around, repenting of their old lives, and heading in a totally new direction. Such was the case for a man named Constantine.

Constantine the Great was the son of Helena, a devout Christian woman, and of Constantius I, king of Rome. When Constantius died, Constantine found himself in a battle for the throne against his enemy, Maxentius. The battle at Milvian Bridge is regarded as a *turning point for Christianity.*[24] After Constantine triumphed over Maxentius, he announced in his speech to dedicate the triumphal arch, that he ascribed his victory not only to the greatness of his imperial genius, but also to the *inspiration of the godhead.*[25] Some said the outcome of the battle was directed by divine providence. Others said that the dead Constantius had personally come to his son's assistance at the head of a heavenly army.

Lactantius, a Christian writer, who was close to Constantine wrote, "Constantine was directed in a dream to cause the heavenly sign (of the cross) to be delineated on the shields of his soldiers… He did as he had been commanded… Having this sign, his troops stood to arms."[26]

Eusebius, the historian, and author of *Church History,* wrote that Constantine had prayed to Jesus Christ for protection before the battle. He prayed that Jesus would reveal to him who he was and would stretch forth his right hand to help him in his present difficulties. While Constantine prayed, a cross of light appeared to him in the heavens, above the sun, and bore the inscription, *CONQUER BY THIS*. He and his whole army, who also witnessed the miracle, were struck with amazement.[27]

While Constantine was still pondering what this sign might mean, night came upon him, and he fell asleep. And he dreamed a dream.

In the dream Jesus appeared to him with the same sign which he had seen in the sky and commanded him to make a likeness of it and to use it as a safeguard in all engagements with his enemies.

When he awoke at dawn, he told the dream to his friends. Calling together the workers in gold and precious stones, he described to them the figure of the sign he had seen. This sign became the insignia of the Christian emperors.

Later, Constantine ordered a cross placed in the hand of the statue erected to him, with an inscription stating that he owed the victory to this symbol. It was also said that St. Helena, Constantine's mother, visited Jerusalem on the inspiration of a dream and so was led to discover the true cross.

## Conclusion

Please note that in the instances of Monica, Augustine's mother, Juddua the high priest, the official, and Constantine, they were all drawing nearer to God in prayer. Shortly afterward, their prayers were answered through dreams.

In many other instances, however, God was the instigator of the action. He gave a dream, and the dreamer was dramatically affected. In those instances the dreamer drew nearer to God *after* the dream.

Actually, it doesn't matter whether your dreams draw you nearer to God before or after they occur. It only matters that you not miss an opportunity to use your dreams, which are God-given tools, to draw nearer to Him.

# Chapter 3: Dream Journaling

> Set up for yourself road marks. Place for yourself guideposts; direct your mind to the highway, the way by which you went.
>
> Jeremiah 31:21

Recently at a dream workshop I spoke about the importance of keeping a journal and recording one's dreams, while holding up a one-inch thick black three-ring notebook for all the audience to see. "This is what my annual dream journal looks like. I have thirty-one more at home just like this one."

The audience gasped and stared at me with renewed respect.

Someone told me afterward that it wasn't that they were impressed with my knowledge or with my abilities, but instead it was my discipline they appreciated. People who are interested in dreams and who attend dream workshops know how difficult it is to be faithful in recording one's dreams. But believe me, if I can do it, so can you.

Dreamers have good intentions to keep a dream journal, like all the dream books recommend. Unfortunately, they run short of time, and they sometimes end up scribbling a dream on the back of an envelope dug out of the bottom of their purse on their way to work. Or they jot down the main points of their dream on the back of the grocery list while waiting in line at the market. They may have every intention of transferring their notes to their dream journal later, but it hardly ever happens. Sometimes the notes get lost, thrown out, or forgotten.

Does this describe your journaling methods? At the end of the year is your dream journal lying abandoned on your night stand—empty? Do you feel guilty knowing you should have written down more dreams? Or do you rummage frantically through your pockets or purse searching for your dream notes, stapling a scribbled-on napkin to a sheet of notebook paper and throwing it loosely between the covers of a notebook?

When you treat your dreams with respect, they'll treat you with respect in return—by giving you more and more dream material with which to work. As you continue keeping a dream journal, over time, patterns begin to become clear that were not seen before. Tangles of ideas are unraveled. As you record and read your dreams, a picture begins to form. It becomes clear that there is a connective thread alive below the surface of your life that has been carrying meaning the whole way, although you've been unaware of it. That thread has woven together events, people, and activities in your life in its effort to create the fabric of your life. That inner creativeness happened while you were asleep.

## Treating Your Dreams with Respect?

Treating your dreams with respect means that you give them attention. Don't act as if they matter very little. Commit to remembering them, and only share your dreams with other Christians who also respect their dreams.

Try your very best to understand your dreams. Give them your valuable time and attention. If they require some action to be taken, then do whatever your dreams say to do. Only fully understand, first, what your dreams are saying. Do something special with special dreams.

When it comes to creating your dream journal, don't throw the entries haphazardly into a pile and call it a dream journal. Make your dream journal special. Keep it in a special place. Give it importance.

The significance of treating your dream journal in a special way is not to make a book of great importance. Think *symbolically*. It is *not* about the book. Rather it is what the entries in the book *represent*—messages from God and messages from your soul that play a significant role in making you whole. That is what is worthy of your respect.

## What Is a Dream Journal?

A dream journal is a record of your dreams, your dream interpretations, your dream drawings, your ideas about your dreams, and your conclusions about your dreams. You might want to think of it as your *dream workbook* since it is the place where you actually do your dream *work*.

Your dream journal is a place where you should be free to be totally honest about your feelings and about your relationships with yourself and with God. No one else should ever have access to your dream journal, unless you give them permission. For instance, you might want to show parts of your journal to your spiritual director. Or you may want to share a few dreams with a special Christian friend who wants to get started on her own dream journal. Although I show the outside of my journals to other people, I rarely show the entries to anyone.

## What Is Your Style of Dream Journal?

There are as many styles of dream journals as there are dreamers. Each dreamer creatively *connects* with his or her own style of dream work. Some keep written dream journals in spiral notebooks, some in three-ring looseleaf binders. Others buy beautifully decorated blank journal books with flowery covered bindings.

Some dream journalers write in longhand script, some type their entries on typing paper and punch holes along the side. Others type their dreams on the computer and keep their entries in computer files or saved on CDs.

Some dreamers record their dreams on audio cassette tapes. Afterward, they insert the tapes into notebooks in the pockets of clear plastic pages. Others might simply rubber band their tapes together according to years.

If you keep your journal saved on memory sticks, your dream journal could be a notebook containing plastic pages with pockets for holding the sticks. The same is true for CDs. Those disks might be labeled individually according to years, such as 2010 Dream

Journal, 2011 Dream Journal, and so forth. Your individual entries might include your interpretation sheets (more about that later), your computer generated dream artwork created from computer graphics, freehand drawn pictures, or pie graphs showing how many dreams repeated during the year.

With computer technology at your fingertips, you could keep tables and graphs of how many dreams you remember per night, or how many times you dream of a certain symbolic figure during a year's time. Or how many dreams contained the same subject matter.

However you decide to journal your dreams, individualize the journal to comply with your style. Draw original artwork on the outside of the notebook or binder. Add your favorite poems. Use colored markers for your entries. Make your dream journal mean something to you and you alone. It should reflect your unique self and what style of journal you like.

Remember that your dream journal doesn't have to start with January and end with December. It can start and end whenever you want. Maybe you work on *wrapping* up the year of your journal during your annual summer vacation, so begin and end in the month of June. Maybe you like to wrap it up when the auditors come to your office in October, after you've finished with inventory. Or maybe you imagine your birthday to be the start and end of your year.

The point is to individualize your dream journal to make it special to you. Make it pleasant to write in, store tapes in, or slip computer disks into. Also, find a special place to store it. Periodically take past dream journals down from the shelf and flip through them, remind yourself of where you've been and where you're going. Reread how far God has brought you and what He has said to you. Remember what the prophet Jeremiah said, "Direct your mind to the highway–the way by which you went."

## Using Interpretation Sheets to Understand Your Dreams

Whether you write down your dreams or speak them into a recorder, it is important to keep your journal entries similar in format. Otherwise, you may be tempted to ramble on and on and never get to the point. Or you could wander off track altogether and arrive at a wrong conclusion about a dream.

You may, of course, use whatever interpretation form works for you. Be as creative as you want about what is included on the sheet, but I have found that these four items should always be included: the date (including the day of the week), the dream, your interpretation, and your response.

When I began to keep a dream journal in 1980, my interpretation sheet was simple. It included the date, the dream, any symptoms or feelings I felt while the dream was happening, and my analysis. At different times during the last thirty-one years, I've changed those items to include other subjects, such as adding the day of the week to the date.

Following is my current version of the Interpretation Sheet, which I'm convinced contains all the items which are important to me concerning my dreams. Feel free to revise it in any way that will help you better understand your dreams.

## Blank Interpretation Sheet

### Dream Interpretation Sheet

Day of the Week:
Date:

Dream Summary:

Main symbols:

Associations:

Type of Dream:

What Is This Dream Telling Me:

What Is My Response:

The Result:

The *Date* of the dream entry is important, of course—first of all so that you can keep your dreams in order. It also helps keep your dreams fixed in time in your mind. You will be able to go back later and know what was occurring in your waking life that might have triggered such a dream.

The *Day of the Week* is also important, especially when you start to look for patterns in your dream life. You might discover that you have *warning* dreams every first Monday of the month, and that is the day when you visit the hospital. Or maybe you have nightmares every Friday night after having your weekly visit with your parents.

The *Dream Summary* entry is simply where you retell your dream. Remember to write down everything you remember about your dream, including colors. If you only remember a fragment or a feeling, record that as well. Sometimes recording only a fragment can cause a flood to begin of dream recall. Note that Daniel did something very similar in Daniel 7:1, "…Daniel saw a dream and visions in his mind as he lay on his bed, then he wrote the dream down and related the following summary of it."

*Main Symbols* can be either main characters in the dream, main objects in the dream, or main actions in the dream. List as many as you want. These symbols will be your material with which to work when making your free associations.

*Associations* are really *free associations*. Take each main symbol, write it on a piece of paper in the middle of the page, and draw a circle around it. Then, think of what that word means to you, write it off to the side and draw a circle around it, then draw a line from the main symbol to your first association. Keep associating with the main symbol until you have an *Aha!* feeling about what the symbol means. Then move on to the next main symbol.

There are fifteen types of dreams that I identified in chapter two. Look down the list and insert what type you most closely identify your dream with in the *Type of Dream* entry.

After you have identified your main symbols, worked with your free associations, and if you know the type of dream your dream is, ask yourself, "What is this dream telling me?" Sometimes the message is clear. Other times the message may elude you. If it does, continue to ask, "Is there a message here?"

If an answer does not come quickly, spend some time *walking around* in your dream for the rest of the day and maybe the next. Sometimes holding a dream in the back of your mind will help it to incubate and then sort of *hatch* into the full-blown picture. If you don't have an answer about what the dream is telling you in a couple of days, then put it out of your mind. Sometimes when you do that, later when you're thinking of something entirely different, the answer will pop up in your mind, and you'll have it.

Once you know what your dream is telling you, a decision should be made. *What is going to be your response?* If a dream tells you to pack and move, will you? That's precisely what happened to Joseph, the husband of Mary, and it didn't happen once. It happened twice. First, in Matthew 2:13-14, the Bible says, "an angel of the Lord appeared to Joseph in a dream, saying, 'Arise and take the Child and His mother, and flee to Egypt, and remain there until I tell you; for Herod is going to search for the Child to destroy Him.' And he arose and took the Child and His mother by night, and departed for Egypt…"

Joseph had a choice *after* he understood the message—to obey or disobey the message. We know that Joseph chose to obey. Will we do the same?

Secondly, Matthew 2:19-22, states, "…an angel of the Lord appeared in a dream to Joseph in Egypt, saying 'Arise and take the Child and His mother, and go into the land of Israel; for those who sought the Child's life are dead.' And he arose and took the Child and His mother, and came into the land of Israel."

The Bible does not say that Joseph wondered about the message, that he questioned the message, or that he hesitated. It says, "And he arose and took the Child…" Obedient and submissive, Joseph took action with his dream. The results brought about God's will for Joseph, for Mary, and for Jesus, the child, not Joseph's will, but God's.

The *Result* entry is very simple. Ask yourself first whether or not you were obedient to your dream's message. Then ask yourself what the result of your action was. You might be surprised at your answer. Sometimes the result is not what you expected at all.

An example of one of Joseph's dreams has been interpreted on the following Dream Interpretation Sheet (the date is imaginary).

# Joseph's Dream on an Interpretation Sheet

## Dream Interpretation Sheet

Day of the Week: Saturday night
Date: On the 21st day of the month of Nissan, 4 A.D.

Dream Summary:
An angel of the Lord appeared to me and said, "Fear not to take Mary for your wife: for that which is conceived in her is of the Holy Ghost. She shall bring forth a son and his name is to be Jesus, for he shall save his people from their sins." Then I woke up.

Main symbols:
Angel of the Lord, Mary, Holy Ghost, a son named Jesus

Associations:
Angel=messenger from God

Type of Dream:
Numinous, comforting, prophetic

What Is This Dream Telling Me:
1) To marry Mary 2) To name the child Jesus

What Is My Response:
When I awoke, I did what the angel of the Lord commanded me. I married Mary.

The Result:
I married Mary, and she had a son, whom I named Jesus. Jesus saved his people from their sins. Dream was fulfilled.

# What Does a Dream Journal Look Like?

Few of us ever get to see someone else's dream journal because dream journalers guard their private space from curious eyes. However, seeing another's dream journal gives us hope that our own dream journal is acceptable and somehow validated. All of a sudden we may think, "Hey, that gives me a good idea!" or, "Wow, I must be on the right track."

If you could see my dream journals you'd see that mine are black three-ring loose-leaf binders with the year written on the spine. On the inside front cover I have taped a plain, white sheet of paper where I track my personal dream symbols for the year.

I personalize the first sheet in the journal by giving the whole journal a short title, such as, *1992—Year of My Healing*; *1985—Year of My Growth;* or *1996—Year of My Seeing*. The page is written in colored markers, freehanded with curlicues and flair, just for my personal amusement.

In addition to my Interpretation Sheets and dream drawings, I place poems I've written about certain dreams and any other journal entries I wish to include. Sometimes I draw simple pictures of my inner spiritual perspective and include those drawings, also.

At the end of each journal for the year I add a sheet of paper with a large circle drawn on it, which is divided like a clock, only instead of numbers, there are names of months. The diagram looks very much like a pie graph, with lines drawn from the center out past the curve of the circle. And on each line I write the date and a main event that occurred on that day. This graph gives me an instant view of the year, showing which months were active and which months were quiet.

The following page is an actual page from one of my dream journals along with its accompanying dream drawing. Feel free to copy it and use it as a sample for your own dream work.

3/18/83 Dream Record

Fragment

Dream Summary: We were moving in the dream, just like we are in reality. There were boxes stacked in the kitchen, and we were carrying boxes outside to a truck. Bill (my husband) was outside at the truck and I came back into the kitchen. As I approached the refrigerator I noticed a sign posted there for me. It said merely: SERVE.

Symptoms/Feelings: None

Analysis: I think this dream means exactly what it says--that I am to serve God more than I do. And my things are packed and ready to go wherever he sends me.

Dream Drawing:

## Another example from my dream journals:

2/10/83 <u>Dream Record</u>

Dream Summary: There were two women with me, one brunette and one blond. We were at a place where it had rained, so the ground was muddy and wet. We went inside a restroom, like at a service station, and there was about four inches of water on the floor. We thought it was very filthy. Then three men drove up. One had black hair, one brown hair, and one blond. We all paired off with the other person of the same color hair. I was with the man with black hair. Then the dream shifted scenes, and we were on a redwood deck looking out over some water. We talked and talked and fell in love. When the men had to leave, he came over to me, looked at me with very loving eyes, and touched my face. He said that he would love to marry me, but that it just wouldn't work out because I was too stubborn, that I always wanted everything my way. It didn't make him stop loving me, but he couldn't stay. He had to go away. He said for me to remember him always, because he loves me.

Symptoms: Feelings of comfort with my women friends. Feelings of warmth and love from the man. Sadness because he had to leave.

Analysis: This man is some part of me. He is disciplining me with his instruction. So, I must look at myself and see where I'm being stubborn and selfish in my life. In what areas do I always want my own way? How am I being stubborn? At the moment I don't know.

<u>Dream Drawing:</u>

I love you, but you're too stubborn.

At some time in your life you may have a dream about dying. Try not to be overly concerned about a death dream. It doesn't necessarily mean anything is physically wrong with you. If you are in good health or if you've had a physical checkup with your doctor, but you are still concerned about the dream, please try to interpret it. With understanding of a dream, often comes peace.

Very often a person who dreams of death will soon dream a dream about birth, meaning that some part of their inner selves has died, some part is re-born. It could be an old ambition, something you've finally turned loose of.

The following dream is an example of a birth dream following a death dream:

11/27/82 Dream Record

Dream Summary: I was pregnant in the dream. When I got to my car, my dad was waiting for me. I told him that I thought I needed to go to the hospital, so I could be checked. I thought I might be having the baby because it seemed extra heavy, but I wasn't having contractions. When we got to the hospital, I told the nurse that I thought I might be having the baby. She took me to a small room with four beds. There were elderly people in all of the beds. So I stood next to the wall and waited for someone to leave. When they left, I laid down. The nurse came in to check me and said it was time for the baby to be born. I protested, saying that I was not experiencing any pain. But she reached between my legs and grasped the baby by the feet and pulled. I felt a huge tug, and she pulled the baby out of me. She said it was a girl, and I started crying. She propped the baby up on the end of the bed for me to see, while she went to get the doctor. When I looked at the baby, she looked just like me, only smaller. Then she lifted up one hand and waved to me and smiled. I waved back and cried tears of happiness.

Symptoms: Happy, elated, puzzled about no labor pains.

Analysis: This dream is very clear to me. It tells me that some part of me has been re-born, fresh, all new. This makes me happy. I guess I would have expected for there to be some "growth" pain with this re-birth, but there's none.

Dream Drawing:

## What Are the Benefits of a Dream Journal?

Keeping a dream journal reaps many benefits throughout the years. First of all, our entries *reveal inner thoughts and feelings about life* that might have previously been hidden to us. Dreams very often reveal attitudes we didn't realize we possessed.

Second, a dream journal, kept over time, could *reveal dormant talents and gifts.*

Third, Louis M. Savary, Patricia H. Berne, and Strephon Kaplan Williams, in their book, *Dreams and Spiritual Growth* say that, "a dream journal *highlights our transition points* in our lives and helps us understand adversities in the light of our larger destiny."[28]

Fourth, a dream journal *reveals to us personal dream symbols* in our lives that we can relate to while on our journey.

Fifth, a dream journal can become *a useful tool of spiritual-discipline,* keeping us faithfully working on our inner lives and listening to God.

Sixth, keeping a dream journal helps us *realize that there is a God* who speaks to us through our dreams, who wants a relationship with us. It gives us a large perspective on who we are and whose we are. We learn through revelation experience with our dreams that there is a God who deeply wants us to draw nearer to him. We come to understand that there is someone *out there* wanting to communicate with us.

Seventh, a dream journal can do what the prophet Jeremiah said. It can *set up road marks and guideposts* along our journey to *keep us focused* on the highway. It can also *remind us where we've been* and *reveal to us where God is leading*.

God said in Jeremiah 33:3, "Call to Me and I will answer you, and I will tell you great and mighty things, which you do not know." God speaks to us through many avenues, such as sermons, scripture, Christian music, the beauty of creation, Christian friends, and sometimes bumper stickers and billboards. God loves you so much; He'll use any means He can, even your dreams, to get you to draw nearer to Him!

# Chapter 4: How People In the Bible Used Their Dreams to Draw Nearer to God

> How much there is in the Bible about dreams! There are, I think, some sixteen chapters in the Old Testament and four or five in the New in which dreams are mentioned; and there are many other passages scattered throughout the book which refer to visions. If we believe the Bible, we must accept the fact that, in the old days, God and his angels came to humans in their sleep and made themselves known in dreams.[29]
>
> Abraham Lincoln
> Fourteenth president of the
> United States of America

Abraham Lincoln was right. There are a lot of dreams in the Bible. Some of us know it. Some of us are surprised to learn about it. Reading about other people's dreams is fascinating. It's sort of like looking through someone else's desk drawer. You know everyone else has one but getting to look at it is very privileged. Only a few get to hear something so personal as another person's dream. Whenever you start talking about a dream, notice how other people begin to gather around and stand to listen. Not that they want to add anything or share. They just want to hear about it. It's almost like hearing a secret. Everyone is curious.

Since everyone is so curious about dreams it is still surprising that very few Christians go look up and read all the dreams in the Bible. It is a fascinating journey. You may think, "Their dreams are more religious than mine. My dreams are just ordinary." It may be true that your dreams have different content than people in the Bible, just because we live differently. It is not because God has changed or because dreaming is different. It is mostly because we are overwhelmed with technology, noise, and stress. If we were quiet and had more solitude, like many of the people in the Bible, then we would be able to hear our dreams much more clearly. If we were more God-centered, our dreams would also reflect that mirror image of numinous dream characters.

If you take the challenge to read the dreams in the Bible, please start with the most powerful dreams first. The dreams of Jacob, Joseph, Daniel, and Joseph, the husband of Mary, are very powerful dreams. They are people who put into action drawing nearer to God because of their dream lives. Let them be a witness and a mentor to you as you practice listening to your dreams.

## Jacob

One of the most famous dreams in the Bible was given to Jacob (Genesis 28:12-15). His dream about the ladder reaching to heaven has been depicted in the artist William Blake's watercolor *Jacob's Ladder*, in folk art toys, in statues, and many other art forms. What is it about the dream that fascinates us so?

The dream figures are certainly interesting and numinous. Dreams with angels, the Lord, and a glimpse of heaven are something we never forget. Are dreams like these the only ones we consider coming from God? No, they aren't. I consider all dreams as being from God. Why? Because dreams are a form of communication from God to us, even if they seem silly or weird. What may look like an ordinary dream still holds important information for your life and your purpose. Sometimes it takes looking at a series of dreams in order to get the full message from God, but the message is there nonetheless. If God created us and put the mechanism in us for dreaming, then dreams come from Him. He is the originator of dreams. There are no throwaway dreams. Even dreams that frighten us (nightmares) are only sent to heal us.

Jacob's dream was a promise dream. The Lord told Jacob in the dream that the land on which he lay would be his and his descendants'. Blessings are overflowing in the dream. God promises Jacob that his descendants will be like the dust of the earth. But maybe the biggest blessing and promise of all is that "all the families of the earth will be blessed" through him. Think about that for a moment. Does *all* mean you and your family? Yes, it does. Therefore, you and your family were blessed through this dream of Jacob's all those thousands of years ago. Remember there is no time limit on blessings, and there is no time limit on dreams. They transcend time. If you have a dream when you are a child, and there's a promise from God in it, then that promise is still good today.

The story of Isaac, Jacob, and Esau in Genesis 25-28 is an interesting family story full of love, deceit, sorrow, blessings, and forgiveness. Not unlike our own family histories. It is comforting to know that God is with us, and He sees what happens in our family. He loves us so much that He will find a way to bless us. But we must be open to hearing Him no matter how He chooses to speak to us.

What do we do if we have a dream like Jacob's? I hope we do not ignore it. Or carry it around in our hearts forever and do nothing with it. When Jacob woke up, he immediately drew nearer to God and declared, "The Lord is in this place, and I did not know...How awesome is this place!...This is none other than the house of God, and this is the gate of heaven" (Genesis 28:16). He built a pillar of stones and anointed it with oil as a remembrance and a tribute. He also changed the name of the city where he had slept from Luz to Bethel. What would you do with such a dream?

Perhaps you could not change the name of the city where you slept at the time of the dream but there are other actions you could take. Be creative. First of all, write it down. Next, thank God for the dream and ask Him what you should do. Tell the people you trust with your dreams. Find something in the dream to use to bless others. Make outward signs and artwork to bring glory to God. Make changes in your life that will show respect to your dream. When a dream like Jacob's happens to you, you feel that you have been touched by God, and you have been. Tell your story. Give your testimony. Spread the word that God still speaks to His people through dreams.

The power of Jacob's dream changed his life. He used his ladder dream as an opportunity to worship God. As outward and visible signs of the inward grace bestowed on him by God in his dream, Jacob built a monument. Maybe you have a monument inside you that is waiting to be built. Take God's promises and God's dreams and let them speak through your life. Let Him have His voice through you.

## Joseph

If there is anyone in the Bible with an interesting interaction with dreams, it is certainly Joseph. Perhaps it was because he was the son of Jacob or because he was in the line of Isaac. Or perhaps it was because Joseph was sensitive to his inner life. But it is clear from scripture that Joseph had a gift with dreams. When he had the two dreams about his brothers bowing down to him, he made the mistake of sharing those dreams with them (Genesis 37:5-10). The mistake was not in sharing the dreams. It was sharing the dreams with people who had no respect for dreams or their meaning. Let Joseph's mistake be a lesson to all of us.

What the brothers underestimated was the power of dreams! If God sends a prophetic dream, then trust that it will happen. Events may come against it. Circumstances may change along the way. Others may try to prevent what was prophesied from happening. But the power of God is stronger than circumstances and the plans of men. God's word does not go forth without accomplishing what He sends it to do (Isaiah 55:11). When the brothers plotted to kill Joseph in verse 20, they said, "Then let us see what will become of his dreams!" What was said in scorn held no power whatsoever over what God had proclaimed for Joseph's future.

In fact, the dreams had prophesied that the brothers would bow down to Joseph two times. But just as God does sometimes, He goes beyond what we expect, and He does even more than promised. In chapters 42, 43, and 44 Joseph's brothers bow down to him four times! Double what the dreams foretold. The brothers grossly underestimated the power of God and the dreams He sends to lead us and guide us toward His purposes. For the dreams were not the end, they were the means. Dreams in the hand of God propel us in the direction He needs us to go in order to fulfill His desires for our very best. In this instance, Joseph said to his brothers, "And now do not be grieved or angry with yourselves, because you sold me here; for God sent me before you to preserve life..." He goes on to say, "God sent me before you to preserve for you a remnant in the earth, and to keep you alive by a great deliverance" (Genesis 45:7).

As you can see, because of his dreams Joseph arrived at a place he never imagined he would be going doing what he never imagined he would do. What Hebrew boy could imagine that he would end up being second in command in Egypt? You can hear it in Joseph's own words, "...It was not you who sent me here, but God; and He has made me a father to Pharaoah and lord of all his household and ruler over all the land of Egypt" (Genesis 45:8). All of that began with two simple little dreams...that ended up not so simple after all.

All along the way in Joseph's life God led him by his dreams. Even when Joseph was in jail he interpreted two dreams, one for the cupbearer and one for the baker (Genesis 40:5-19). Perhaps those were not the only persons he interpreted dreams for. From my own experience I know that word gets around about you when you talk about dreams. Others are either simply curious about you or they come to you for genuine help with their dreams' meanings. Evidently that happened to Joseph because by the time he got to Pharaoh two years later, Pharaoh said, "I have heard it said about you, that when you hear a dream you can interpret it" (Genesis 41:1-15). His reputation had preceded him. And he did not take credit for such knowledge. Instead he gave all the glory to God. "...God will give Pharaoh a favorable answer," he said. His reward was being put in charge of everything in Egypt.

How did God bless Joseph throughout his life because of his attention to dreams? Most of all he was blessed with the job of being ruler over all of Egypt. That position brought him fame, fortune, reconciliation with his brothers, favor with many, position, respect, authority, and untold blessings. On the other hand, what would have happened if Joseph never paid any attention to his dreams? If, after the first two dreams, he had kept his mouth shut and decided to forget about the dreams, how would his life have been different?

You might think he would have been better off because his brothers would never have sold him into slavery. Maybe. But they were already jealous of him because his father showed favoritism toward him and gave him the coat of many colors. But, for sake of argument, we say the brothers would have all gotten along. If he had more dreams, he would have ignored those, too. Pretty soon, perhaps he would stop remembering any dreams. Or if that didn't happen, if he did keep having dreams, sooner or later he would begin to wonder if they meant anything. Would it be too late for him to cultivate this gift he had been given?

Think of the blessings he would have missed. His life in Egypt would have never happened. His accomplishments for the people of Egypt would have never happened. God would have had to find someone else to save the starving people of Egypt. Joseph would have been missing in action.

Is it a small thing to ignore your dreams? Maybe not today. Maybe not tomorrow. But at some point, I would say "yes," ignoring our dreams holds sad consequences. It is similar to God calling our name and having us turn around and walk away. How can we do that? How can we miss the rich opportunities that God sends our way. Wake up! Wake up and hear your dreams.

## Daniel

Daniel was extraordinary. Like Joseph, he could interpret dreams. In fact he understood dreams so well that the Bible says, "...he could understand all kinds of visions and dreams" (Daniel 1:17). But Daniel's gift went beyond understanding. He had the ability to draw so near to God in prayer that God revealed to him not only understanding of dreams, but also the ability to know what dreams other people dreamed. No other dream worker in all of the Bible could do what Daniel could do.

Because of this unusual gift Daniel eventually told King Nebuchandnezzar's dream to him along with its interpretation. It had come to Daniel in a night vision. Was the night vision a dream? Scripture doesn't say. However, Daniel gave God the glory for revealing the dream and interpretation to him. At first the king received the interpretation with thanksgiving, and he lavished gifts on Daniel and proclaimed him as ruler of all Babylon and chief among all wise men (Daniel 2:47). But then the king did something very wrong. He misused the information in the dream by creating an idol for his subjects to worship. He had spent no time asking God what the dream meant or what God intended him to do with the dream. He did not ponder what the symbols were and what they meant for either his country or his people. He let his ego and his pride rule his reaction to the dream.

In contrast, Daniel drew near to God in prayer with fasting, sackcloth, and ashes. He confessed his own sins and the sins of all the people. Then God began to visit Daniel with angels and prophecies, showing him extraordinary visions of end times. God trusted Daniel with divine revelations because Daniel had proven he could be trusted with his dreams.

Never assume that your dreams are only meant for you or for your own blessings. Most of the time they are. However, sometimes God wants to use you as His instrument, as His hands and feet, to minister to someone else, and He tells you about it in a dream. It is so important that you take what you have written about your dream and work on it in order to make certain that you have it all figured out. Get God involved with the interpretation of your dreams! Ask Him what they mean. Ask Him what He is trying to tell you.

He may give you another dream with an explanation or more information. Or He may send someone to you to answer your questions. Information may come across your path that will shed light on what you were puzzled about. Journal the meaning of the dream. Have a written dialogue with one or two of the dream characters. Look up scriptures that might be connected to what the dream says. Go on a search, like an excavation, digging and digging until the answer is unearthed.

Then when you are satisfied that you know the real meaning, it is time to take appropriate action. Pray. Ask God what the next step is. Then take that step. As we know, sometimes that's all God will give us at a time... the next step. But take it. Even if God is asking you to do something difficult. Daniel had to tell a king to repent of his sins. Most likely your mission will not be that daunting. But whatever it is, be faithful with the dreams you are given. You may be assured that rich blessings await on the other side.

## Joseph, the Husband of Mary

Imagine for a moment you are God. Imagine you are sending your only Son into the world to be born, to live, to fulfill a powerful task, and to die. What sort of man would you choose to be His stepfather? He must be wise. He must be trustworthy. He must be loving and kind. He must be righteous, and it goes without saying, that he must listen to God. He should be obedient, and he should listen to his dreams. Joseph was all of those things… and more.

When his betrothed wife became pregnant, Joseph was not the type of man who lightly tossed her aside. He was a righteous man who did not want to disgrace Mary so he considered what to do. While he was considering his next step he had a dream. Has this ever happened to you? You may be worried over an important decision. You want to do the right thing. But you're back and forth between two alternatives? Then a dream happens. And all of a sudden, it all seems clear. Why hadn't you seen it before? Now you know what needs to be done. And you get up and do it.

That is what Joseph did. After the dream he arose from his sleep, and did what his dream said to do. He married Mary. Did he continue to wonder if it was the right thing to do? Did he talk it over with his friends? No, he didn't. Did he question whether he had heard the dream correctly? No. He had all the information he needed to do the right thing. We all should be so proactive.

Armed with the message from his dream Joseph knew he had a unique mission from God. To raise God's Son and to keep Him safe. How could he do it on his own? He could not. He needed to use every available tool God gave him to accomplish the task.

Joseph was a responsible husband and stepfather. He valued his wife and child. Being the father of "He who will save His people from their sins" (Matthew 1:21) required a meek man. Submissive and compliant could be used to describe Joseph, and his relationship with God. When God warned him in a dream about the danger to the Child and told him to flee to Egypt, he did. Later when God told him the danger was passed, and he should come back to Israel, he did. Has God ever told you specifically in a dream to do a certain thing? Did you obey?

Jesus's life began with dreams being dreamed by people around him. It also ended with someone having a dream about him...Pilate's wife (Matthew 27:19). It seems obvious that God used dreams to speak to people whom He needed to communicate with. Other than Jacob, Joseph, Daniel, and Joseph the husband of Mary, there are many other people in the Bible who dreamed dreams. They shared their dreams, like we do, when they needed answers to what they meant. Some wrote their dreams down, like Daniel. Some obeyed God. Some did not. But in every situation the ones who listened to God in their dreams were blessed.

## Gideon

God can use dreams to encourage us, to fortify us for jobs He gives us to do. In Gideon's situation God put Gideon in a particular place at a particular time in order to overhear someone else's dream and its interpretation in order to empower Gideon to do battle. God told Gideon, "...if you are afraid to go down [against the enemy], go with your servant down to the camp, and you will hear what they say; and afterward your hands will be strengthened..." (Judges 7:10-11). His hands *were* strengthened, and he won the victory over his enemy.

Was the dream Gideon's dream? No, it wasn't. It was obviously a warning dream given to a man in the enemy camp. But Gideon was in the right place at the right time to use the dream to his advantage, and it brought him victory.

Women ask me from time to time whether they should listen to other people's dreams. They feel it is a waste of time since the dream does not apply to them. My advice is always to take the time and listen. You may minister to a friend by receiving revelation knowledge about their dream. At the least you can offer a warm hug and a nod of acknowledgment. You might be surprised, however, when God uses a friend's dream in order to bless you.

## Solomon

What a blessed man Solomon was! Besides the obvious blessing of wealth beyond anyone's imagination, he received two visitations from the Lord in dreams. In one dream God gave him understanding and sound judgment. He also gave him riches and honor and a promise and a long life (1 Kings 3:13-14).

Then later the Lord appeared to him again in a dream and reiterated the Davidic Covenant promising Solomon his kingdom would be established over Israel forever. That dream is found in chapter nine. Sadly, by chapter eleven God is angry with Solomon because he did not obey what God had told him in the two dreams.

Solomon's experience makes us stop and ask ourselves, "Am I still obeying what God told me to do in previous dreams?" I have a friend who believes that God told her to move to a certain city to take care of her aging mother. After ten years of living in a city that she doesn't like from time to time she complains and questions whether she should move away, saying, "Life is passing me by. I need to have a life!" But when asked about her life in the city where God sent her, she lists off blessing after blessing from God that she enjoys where she is. She comes up short when shown that she does indeed have a life, a very good life, exactly where God put her.

## Abimelech and Nightmares

Like my friend, sometimes God saves us from ourselves, and our own selfish desires. When Abimelech, the king, took Sarah, Abraham's wife, by mistake, he had no idea that he was messing around with God's prophet, and there was a promise attached to Abraham. The promise was so strong in that household while

Abraham and Sarah were there all the other women in the house became infertile in order to preserve the child promised to Abraham from Sarah.

So when Abimelech took Sarah, God showed up in a dream and basically said, "I'm going to kill you!" (Genesis 20:3). Now some people might consider this dream a nightmare! But no. It was a dream from God who was preserving Abimelech's life by giving him an opportunity to repent and do the right thing. And who was also protecting His promise to Abraham.

Do nightmares come from God? Or do nightmares come from evil spirits?As I have said many times, I am convinced that all dreams come from God. 1) Because He created us, 2) He put in us the ability to dream, 3) The purpose of dreams is to heal our souls, 4) If we study a series of our dreams it becomes clear that God is trying to tell us something, and 5) God communicated with His people in Bible days through dreams, and He has not changed. He still communicates the same way today.

Is it possible for a nightmare to come from evil spirits? No. I don't believe it is. But let me explain. If the purpose of dreams is to heal us, and it is clear that it is, then dreams are not meant to harm us. *Even though* they may look and act scary! Scary dreams are meant to get our attention. Even God's dream to Abimelech was meant to get his attention. Through the years I have worked with spiritual directees and their dreams, sometimes they will have scary dreams about health problems. They will run to me asking for advice. First, we go over the dream to see what God might be saying. If there is not anything that seems right about our answer, then I recommend a trip to the doctor. Is your body trying to tell you something? A lot of time that will be the answer. If it is not, then we start examining what associations could be made between the illness and the dreamer's awake life. We always find the answer in one of those two places.

Christians tend to give Satan and his angels more credit for power than they actually deserve. Giving dreams to Christians is not something they have the power to do. Remember that Satan is not omniscient. He is not omnipresent. He is not omnipotent. He does not have unlimited powers. One of his limited powers is that he cannot read your thoughts. He only knows what you say, write, and do. Therefore, he cannot read your dreams.

Can he influence your dreams? Yes, because he can influence your awake life... if you let him. If you open a door for Satan to come in, he can have an influence on you. But if you dress yourself in God's armor every day (Ephesians 6), you are dressed for that battle. If you have made Jesus Christ Lord of your life, then you are covered under the blood of Jesus. You are safe from the enemy. If you fill your mind with the Word of God, Satan's influence will have no effect. Never assume that because you have a bad dream that it is coming from evil spirits. Do not give them that much credit! Write your dream down and pray over it. Figure out what God is telling you. He will make it clear because He wants you to know what He says.

Conversely, God, Jesus, and the Holy Spirit can certainly have influence over the dreams of *unbelievers*, and those dreams can most certainly be nightmares to the unrighteous! For instance, Pontus Pilate's wife was very upset because of a nightmare she had. It was early in the morning when the chief priests and elders led Jesus away to Pilate. We can only suppose that when Pilate's wife awoke that morning from the nightmare, she discovered from her servants that her husband was at that moment sitting in judgment of the man in her dream. She was so upset she sent a message to her husband while he was at work.

Pilate, who received her message, was sitting on the judgment seat at the time presiding over the trial of Jesus. He had his hands full with the chief priests and elders on one hand begging for blood, and the man, Jesus, on the other hand who seemed totally innocent to him. In the middle of all that stress Pilate received the message from his wife saying, "Have nothing to do with that righteous Man; for last night I suffered greatly in a dream because of Him" (Matthew 27:19). What would most husbands do in that situation? Would they stop their work if they got a note from their wives about a nightmare she had? Probably not. Most likely they'd wait until they got home from work to listen to what she had to say. Was God sending Pilate's wife a message? A warning dream from God in the form of a nightmare to get her attention? A foretelling perhaps of what was to come. It seems so because in a couple of scriptures later Pilate asks, "Then what shall I do with Jesus?" Had God already sent Pilate the answer to that question through the dream of his wife? I don't think we'll know the answer to that until the Hereafter. But if there was any time in history when a man should have listened to a dream, it was surely at that precise moment!

## Challenge

If you are interested in dreams and how God might talk to you through yours, I would challenge you to read the dreams in the Bible. I hope it will open your eyes to the fact that God has used dreams to talk to His people throughout history, and He is still doing it today. If you shut Him out in your waking life, please do not shut Him out in your dreams. Like Abraham Lincoln said, "If we believe the Bible, we must accept the fact that, in the old days, God and his angels came to humans in their sleep and made themselves known in dreams." Meditate on how He made Himself known thousands of years ago. Your dream life is a fertile field of a Way to have God in your life every day. He will not withhold Himself from you. You can begin to hear God speak to you today through His Word and through the dreams of the Bible.

# Chapter 5: Creating Something Real from Something Symbolic

I dream my paintings and then I paint my dreams.

Vincent Van Gogh
Dutch Post-Impressionist Artist

My holy dream is White.
I never dream in white.

I am in a house with relatives all around.
Awake, I know them not.

There is much ado over making supper.
… "Yes, I'll get more plates."
Up the stairs, to the left,
Just past the Empty Room.
White plates in a White cabinet.

With plates stacked under my chin,
I scoot down the hallway.
The Empty Room seems brighter now.
I gingerly peek in.
And…there He is,
Standing in a mist of white

With arms raised up in prayer
And His eyes gazing up to the Father.
I stand in awe and stare. Only stare.

My eyes have dried open.
…I cannot blink.
They are two hot coals in my face.
…I must not blink.
Hot tears burn trenches down both my cheeks,
And drip onto the plates I hold.
…I…will…not…blink.

Do I fall to my knees?
I cannot move. I only stare.
Do I dare to speak?
I cannot.

I finally whisper
Almost silently…

"Lord, is that You?"
And He answers,
"I Am."[30]

Do dreams really come true? The surprising answer to that age-old question is: yes! In fact, they *already are* true.

Dreams never lie to us. They feed us information that is absolutely true about ourselves, our world, and our God. Yet, sometimes it is hard for us to believe such information because it doesn't seem to *fit* our experiences.

And as hard as we try, sometimes a dream won't seem to fit with either who we are or what we do. We may walk around in a dream for weeks, months, or years with the nagging sensation that there's something just not right.

When we struggle with ill-fitting dreams, it often helps to create something else that does make sense in order to understand the dream that doesn't make sense. That *something else* might be as simple as drawing a picture of your dream, or drawing a sketch of only one small symbol from the dream. It might help to write a poem, like the one above, which I wrote using a dream as my inspiration.

If it's difficult for you to think small, you may want to create something complex, such as a fine painting, an epic poem, a sculpture, or a wood carving. Or, if you're an architect, it could be as bold as a building design, or something in between.

Whether the work is simple or complex or somewhere in between, the work used in creating something real from something symbolic contains powerful spiritual energy. Such spiritual energy soon makes the dream come alive in a way that is both comprehensible and tangible.

In the creating process you enter into action similar to copying God, the Creator, when He made something from nothing. It is comparable to what Jesus said in John 5:19, "...for whatever the Father does, these things the Son also does in like manner." And the end result is that the spiritual energy you exert transforms into a form of worship.

You may say, "But I can't draw!" or, "I'm not an artist." That may be true. Your drawing may look like a first grader's, your clay figure may be lopsided, but expert art is not the goal. The artwork you create may never be seen by another human being, but it will contain powerful spiritual energy for you for a long time. It is seen by God, however, and by its very nature, is an acknowledgment that you created as a response to His attempt to bring you to wholeness.

## Rational and Creative Thoughts

Connie and I met together every Thursday morning for a year. Her goal for the year was to become more disciplined in her spiritual life. She contacted me by phone, and I agreed to meet with her. As part of my spiritual direction for Connie, I asked her to write down her dreams so we could discover more about her interior life.

One morning I asked Connie to draw a simple drawing of one of her dreams for me. Hesitantly, she chose a colored marker and began to draw. After a few minutes she sat back and stared at the simple finished picture in her hands. "I never saw that before now," she explained. "Wow, that's amazing!"

Connie had discovered what many people discover who draw their dreams—that you know much more than you think you do. When your rational thoughts compute as far as they can go with the information they've been given, they stop. And you may think, "Well, I can't figure this out. I'm quitting." But if you can access your creative thoughts, they can then take over and feed you additional non-rational or intuitive ideas that you never knew were possible.

To tap into your creative thoughts, sometimes it takes only a tiny action, such as picking up a colored marker and drawing a line on a page, to liberate you from the cage of limited knowledge into a world of free-flying revelation knowledge. And where *Wow!* is the spontaneous reaction.

When your creative thoughts take flight, they may create something that your rational thoughts say is *useless nonsense*. But, at the finish, that creative work feeds manifold information to your rational mind, astounding it with the absolute truth it has revealed. This method of teaching was used many times by Jesus as he used creative picture stories (parables) to teach others profound truths.

Rational thoughts are composed of abstract judgment, analytical ideas, successive relationships, and in-time experiences. Creative thoughts are different. Creative thoughts contain intuition, imagination, symbolism, and revelation. Understanding your dreams utilizes both of these thought processes; thus, Connie's reaction to her drawing. Her creative thoughts drew the picture, and her rational thoughts recognized the truth.

Now let's take a look at Connie's dream and her drawing:

> I was with my ex-husband on a Ferris wheel. The compartments on the Ferris wheel were large enough to stand in, so he and I stood, looking out as the Ferris wheel started going up. The higher the Ferris wheel went the more

> afraid I became. I said, 'I don't like this a bit.' He put his arm around me, and I sort of snuggled down in his arm and felt warm and safe, very comfortable. I was no longer afraid.

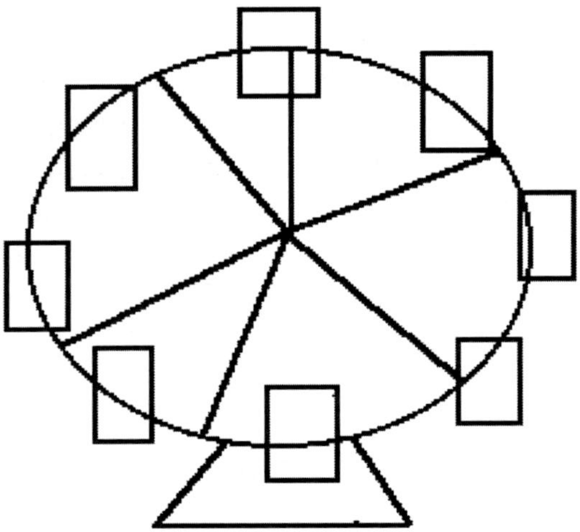

I asked Connie, "What does your ex-husband symbolize to you?"

She answered, "My old life. In some ways it was safe and comfortable. In other ways it was a wild ride. Either way, it was familiar. I knew what to expect."

"What is scaring you about your new life?"

"I guess my new life is sort of unknown. I'm really having to get out of my comfort zone to begin a life with Jesus. This is a *higher* way of life for me, and I want it with all my heart, but it's also a little scary—just because I don't know what God is going to do with me."

Connie's dream revealed to her that fear was keeping her from trusting Jesus totally with her life. After understanding the problem, Connie and I were able to pray about her fear and about her hesitation to trust, and she was set free to follow Jesus wherever He leads.

## Dreams Reveal Unknown Thoughts

One of the benefits of understanding our dreams is that dreams can reveal ideas or thoughts that were previously unknown. Such a dream happened to me on March 12, 1983:

> I was traveling up the incline on Interstate Highway 20 on my way to work. I take this route to work every morning. In the dream I am pushing a large, green dill pickle, about the size of a sofa, down the road. I am in the third lane from the right, and I'm trying to move into the far right lane in order to exit onto the feeder road. I work my way carefully across the lanes of traffic and start up the feeder road, which is a steep incline. I've been very careful not to get hit by all the cars on the highway. It is difficult work.

Seemingly, this is a crazy and comical dream. One that most people would call me and say, "You won't believe the stupid dream I had last night!" Fortunately, through experience, I've learned that dreams are never stupid. They just sometimes look ridiculous on the surface.

In order to understand this dream fully, I needed to create a drawing depicting the giant green pickle and the busy highway. As I drew, I realized that the highway represented my journey through life, and that on my journey I constantly avoid colliding with other people. The giant dill pickle symbolized something sour in my life I was trying to move off to the side, off my main road.

By the time I finished drawing the pickle, I realized, *Wow!* The sour thing in my life, I learned, was my relationship with a coworker who constantly caused problems for me on the job. Unconsciously I had tried to pacify my coworker by passivity and avoidance. But the dream revealed that I needed to be more proactive in moving her out of my path.

The following drawing, depicting my pickle dream, reveals its positive outcome:

# Inspiration for a Potter

Donna, a Christian friend and artist, called to say, "Help! I need to know what a dream means. Ask me some questions!"

She excitedly shared her dream:

> A woman took out a vessel. She asked me if I would like to drink out of the vase, which was full of water. I said yes. But when I drank from it, the rim bent. The clay was still soft, so I just pushed and molded it back to its original shape with my finger. It had grapes and leaves on it, and was well crafted, but still in the soft clay phase.

I asked, "What is a vessel?"

Donna replied, "This one was a vase filled with water."

"Okay, but what is it a symbol of?"

"I don't have the slightest idea."

"Well, let's look in the Bible," I suggested. Second Timothy 2:20-21, was found, and I read it to Donna, "Now in a large house there are not only gold and silver vessels, but also vessels of wood and of earthenware (clay), and some to honor and some to dishonor. Therefore, if a man cleanses himself from these things (wickedness), he will be a vessel for honor, sanctified, useful to the Master, prepared for every good work."

Donna and I continued to talk, and she discovered that the clay vessel was a symbol of her life and that the water in the vase symbolized the cleansing that Jesus had done for her. Then she pondered the grapes and leaves on the vessel remembering what Jesus said in John 15:5 NAS, "I am the vine, you are the branches…"

Donna commented, "It reminds me that the vine on the vase is like my life being clothed with Christ."

She also recognized that the soft clay symbolized her *moldability* and when asked, "What is this dream telling you?"

She responded, "I'm a clay vessel, clothed with Christ that is still being molded by God, the Potter."

Later she called to say that she'd been creating a vase on her potter's wheel exactly like the one in her dream. Donna added, "It'll be a constant reminder of how God is still molding me into something useful for Him."

## "I Am the Bread"

Sally started her own bakery shop five years ago, and today ships her breads and muffins all across America, plus Europe. "God has been good to me," she says with a beaming smile. "I now receive the *whole* loaf!"

What may seem like gibberish to some was like music to my ears. You see, six years ago while Sally was still baking cookies in her kitchen for relatives and friends, she had a dream. Not an action dream with characters and motion, but a voice-only dream, giving her direction. The voice said, *"I offer you the whole loaf, but you only take the crumbs!"*

"I knew it was God," Sally stated emphatically. "No doubt about that. What I didn't know was what it meant."

"I lost sleep over that dream," she said. "I thought about how my life was crumby, thinking that might be it. But still it just didn't feel right. I didn't really begin to get the true picture until I read God's Word and made that first loaf of bread."

"I decided after days of questioning what bread meant to finally look it up in the Bible. That's when I found where Jesus said, '…it is my Father who gives you the true bread out of heaven. For the bread of God is that which comes down out of heaven, and gives life to the world…I am the bread of life…' (John 6:32-33,35). Well, that hit me like a ton of bricks!

"That night I stayed up all night making loaves of bread. I got out every recipe I had on bread making. I made big loaves, little loaves, and twisted loaves. I had bread everywhere! And I got the biggest thrill out of kneading that dough between my fingers and of the aroma that filled my house when it baked. And that's when the light turned on!"

"Wow!" I said.

Sally added, "Just like this bread fills all of my senses, so Jesus can do in my life! He can satisfy every hunger! My dream changed my life forever. No longer will I just accept crumbs that are thrown my way. I am only satisfied now with receiving the *whole* loaf that Jesus holds out for me to take."

From those first few loaves of bread baked in Sally's kitchen in the middle of the night grew a very profitable bakery business. When Sally made something real out of something symbolic, by creating her bread business, she began sharing Jesus all around the world.

## A Scientific Dream

Even scientists listen to their dreams and create something real from something symbolic, thus creating scientific solutions. In 1869, Dmitri Mendeleyev, a professor of chemistry at Saint Petersburg, went to bed after trying unsuccessfully to visualize a way to classify chemical elements based upon their atomic weights. Then Dmitri had a dream.

He reported, "I saw in a dream a table where all the elements fell into place as required."

Awakening, he immediately wrote the dream down on a piece of paper. Only in one place did he later make a necessary correction. As a result of this dream, Dmitri created the periodic table of elements, which is still taught in many science classes throughout the world.[31]

## Nebuchadnezzar's Misunderstood Dream Image

The most notably misunderstood dream work in the Bible is the image that Nebuchadnezzar, King of Babylon, created from his dream about the statue. As you'll recall from the book of Daniel, Nebuchadnezzar dreamed about a large statue made of multi-metallic elements: the head being gold, the arms and chest silver, the belly and thighs bronze, the legs iron, and the feet partly iron and partly clay. In the dream a stone crushed the statue so completely that not even a trace remained (Daniel 2:31-36).

After seeking desperately for an interpretation, Daniel revealed the true answer and the following symbolism to Nebuchadnezzar:

- The multi-metallic elements symbolized five kingdoms, Nebuchadnezzar being the golden kingdom
- The great mountain symbolized God's everlasting kingdom
- The stone symbolized what would later be revealed as the cornerstone—Jesus Christ

Nebuchadnezzar, delighted with the interpretation, let his enthusiasm lead him to make a grave error in judgment. Rather than creating a work of art in thanksgiving for the stone (the coming Savior), he created a work of art in thanksgiving to the golden kingdom—his own kingdom!

Once the statue he created was set up on the plane of Dura in the province of Babylon, Nebuchadnezzar assembled all of his governmental leaders at the dedication where it was announced that when "…you hear the sound of the horn…you are to fall down and worship the golden statue…" (Daniel 3:5). And, of course, when Shadrach, Meshach, and Abed-nego—Daniel's friends—refused to comply, Nebuchadnezzar threw them into the fiery furnace, which he'd ordered heated seven times hotter than usual (Daniel 3:19).

Later when he saw them loosened from their bonds and walking in the blazing furnace, he must have felt utterly humiliated. In the face of God's mighty power at work, Nebuchadnezzar finally did what he should have done in the first place; he created something that brought glory to God. He created a proclamation which declared to all people the signs and wonders God had done for him (Daniel 4:37).

The proclamation, *not* the golden statue, more adequately portrayed God's hand at work in Nebuchadnezzar's dreams. As he proclaimed, "For His dominion is an everlasting dominion, and His kingdom endures from generation to generation" (Daniel 4:34), he was really proclaiming, "God revealed to me in a dream that my kingdom is passing away, but His will last forever."

## Inspiration for Creating a Job

When Joseph revealed to Pharaoh the meaning of his dream about the famine in Egypt, he was also inspired with a creative solution to the problem. The answer was simple. Create a job, hire a man to be in charge, and stockpile grain. The idea was brilliant!

Even Pharaoh recognized a good idea when he saw one—create something real from something symbolic. He knew it would take a God-inspired man to be in charge of all the food in Egypt, and he knew Joseph was that man. He said, "…there is no one so discerning and wise as you are" (Genesis 41:39).

So Joseph created his job according to what Pharaoh's dreams foretold. During the seven years of plenty, he stored up a fifth of the produce of the land. And when the famine arrived, it ravaged all the land, except Egypt (Genesis 41:25-54). Joseph and Pharaoh's cooperative efforts became powerful spiritual energies, resulting in not only the saving of a nation, but also the saving of Joseph's relationships with his family members.

It seems that while Joseph related the interpretation to Pharaoh, his creative thoughts sprouted wings. When the problem was revealed in the interpretation, a ready solution had already taken flight in Joseph's mind. When rational thoughts are set aside in favor of creative work, unimaginable solutions in the form of revelation knowledge flood in to bless, convert, and save. Doing creative dream work puts you in God's hands where He empowers you with His ideas and His wisdom—where He can tell you great and mighty things that you do not know (Jeremiah 33:3).

# Chapter 6: God Is a God of Symbols

> Now listen, Joshua the high priest, you and your friends who are sitting in front of you—indeed they are men who are a symbol, for behold, I am going to bring in My servant the Branch.
>
> Zechariah 3:8

My friend, Sheila, confided that she wanted to attend a liturgical church on Ash Wednesday. "It just seems to mean more with the imposition of ashes," she said. So I directed her to a parish church very near and dear to my heart. Not knowing whether she was familiar with the formal traditions I waited for her to ask questions. When she didn't ask, I assumed she knew what she would encounter in a liturgical setting.

On Thursday morning I received an email that read, "I should have studied up on the symbols before I went. It would have helped me understand the service better." My heart sank. I should have explained the service with all of its symbols to her instead of assuming she knew. I forget that not all churches enjoy the rich traditions and full flavor of God's symbolism. And Sheila wasn't a regular member of a liturgical church. At the same time I thought that covering all of the symbols of the church service might be a little overwhelming. "What do I explain and what do I leave out?" I asked myself.

There are candles, crosses, vestments with all of their parts, altars, incense, holy anointing oil, unleavened bread, wine, and of course, that day, ashes on the forehead. In a liturgical church, while kneeling on a kneeler in the quiet of the nave, one can look around and ask a million questions. What's that? What does that mean? Why are they doing that? Over time a congregant learns the names of every item in the church, what it is called, and what it is a symbol of. But why would God and/or the Church fill the worship service with so many symbols? The reasonable answer is: because God is a God of symbols.

What exactly is a symbol? The short version is, a symbol is "a visible sign of something invisible."[32] If I were to change that definition for my own spiritual satisfaction, I would say that a symbol is a visible *picture* of something invisible. A symbol is something we can perceive with our five senses. We can touch, see, hear, smell, or taste a symbol. We can't touch, see, hear, smell, or taste something that is invisible.

It is only logical then that God would try to communicate to us through our senses what He cannot show us from His invisible, spiritual world. For instance, when Jesus was trying to explain what the Spirit was like in the Gospel of John, it tells us that Jesus used the symbol of flowing water to convey the picture of what the invisible Spirit is like. Jesus said, "If any man is thirsty, let him come to Me and drink. He who believes in Me, as the Scripture said, 'From his innermost being shall flow rivers of living water.' But this He spoke of the Spirit, whom those who believed in Him were to receive; for the Spirit was not yet given, because Jesus was not yet glorified" (John 7:37-39).

Flowing waters—they knew what flowing waters were like. They had seen that. But what must the Holy Spirit be like? They had not seen that. They didn't know anyone who had seen it who could describe it to them. It was invisible. But Jesus had seen it. He knew it well. He could show them a symbol of what its characteristics were like. Then they sort of understood. They could get a faint grasp of what it might feel like, what it might look like.

When God wanted Moses to build the tabernacle, He had a lot of explaining to do in order to figuratively draw Moses a picture of the dwelling place He had in mind. Because when God told Moses to tell the sons of Israel to raise a contribution to construct a building, God was actually showing Moses symbols of the New Jerusalem that were and still are invisible to man. When God said, "...let them construct a sanctuary for Me, that I may dwell among them" (Exodus 25:8), Moses had no idea what He was talking about. God was about to describe something to Moses that was totally foreign to his imagination.

The pattern God was going to give Moses was a symbol, a visible sign of something invisible to Moses. Not only was the building itself a symbol, but everything in the building was a symbol. From the furniture to the fabrics everything had a meaning. There was nothing in the tabernacle that was not a symbol for something heavenly. We know that because in Revelation 21:2-3, when John saw the heavenly vision, he saw a new heaven and a new earth. He said, "I saw the holy city, new Jerusalem, coming down out of heaven from God… And I heard a loud voice from the throne, saying 'Behold, the tabernacle of God is among men, and He shall dwell among them, and they shall be His people, and God Himself shall be among them.'"

Therefore, the pattern that Moses received on the mountain was the symbol; all of it was symbols, of the holy city which will come down out of heaven at the end of the ages. Of course, Moses built the tabernacle as God directed. Every last detail was crafted according to God's plan. Nothing just happened. It was all deliberate, and everything meant something.

## God's Most Important Symbols

In the church God speaks clearly to His people with two very important symbols: the unleavened bread and the wine. Jesus said of the wine, "This is my blood of the covenant which is poured out for many for forgiveness of sins…" For Jesus, the wine perfectly represented His blood. Therefore, why would we want to change what He had already made perfect? If we believed what Jesus said wouldn't we be more specific about using the same elements that He used? Wouldn't we be more hesitant to substitute what He used with something weaker… i.e. grape juice? Today, the use of unfermented grape juice for communion is the standard practice for most Protestant churches. However, few know the origins of this custom that dates back to 1869 with Thomas Bramwell Welch, MD (1825-1903), the founder of Welch's grape juice.

Welch was the first person to stop the natural fermentation of wine by applying Louis Pasteur's pasteurization process to Concord grape juice. He developed this "alcohol-free wine" specifically for use in the church where he was the communion steward in Vineland, New Jersey. Initially, Welch's grape juice was intended solely for communion in the church. Throughout his life he was an outspoken temperance activist and fought against the effects of alcohol. By 1893 Welch's grape juice became a national favorite as thousands sampled it at the Chicago World's Fair. Possibly it was the World's Fair that brought the cultural acceptance of grape juice to the church.[33] This was an innovative idea at a time when churches typically poured fermented wine out of a pitcher and into a large *common cup* or chalice. But in 1882 in Brooklyn, New York, Mr. A. Van Derwerken wrote an article advocating using individual cups in the communion service. The following year the Psi Upsilon fraternity in Rochester, New York, celebrated the Lord's supper with individual cups. The idea of serving communion in what looked like a *shot glass* didn't catch on right away as few parishioners saw the need for such innovation.[34] Both of these modern day innovations may have had a use and, in and of themselves, do not seem wrong. But what they do is alter what God set forth as the elements that He wanted, which held a higher symbolic message and a higher sacramental meaning.[35]

When Jesus gave out the unleavened bread, He said, "Take, eat. This is My body" (Matthew 26:26, Mark

14:22, Luke 22:19). But He goes on in John's gospel to emphasize how essential eating the bread is. He said:

> ...Unless you eat the flesh of the Son of Man and drink His blood, you have no life in yourselves. He who eats My flesh and drinks My blood has eternal life, and I will raise him up on the last day. For My flesh is true food, and My blood is true drink. He who eats My flesh and drinks My blood abides in Me and I in him (John 6:54-56).

But what kind of bread should be used to represent His body? Some people say it doesn't matter. But it must matter to God. Otherwise He would not have been so specific in Exodus 12:17-20 about what kind of bread it should be. God said unleavened bread. And then God called that day the Feast of Unleavened Bread (Exodus 12:17). I submit that the bread that is a symbol for His Body should be the same that is used for the Passover meal–unleavened bread. Some may say that using unleavened bread is following the Law, but that's not true. The apostle Paul, in 1 Corinthians 5:8, encouraged the mostly gentile church there to "celebrate the feast, not with old leaven, nor with the leaven of malice and wickedness but with the unleavened bread of sincerity and truth." In many churches today unleavened bread consists of stamped wafers cut into circles. Some use small white pillows of unleavened bread. Others use Matza bread, which seems to be a very good symbol of the body of Christ. It is square, flat unleavened bread with stripes baked onto the bread, representing the stripes of Jesus and also has holes punched in it, which represent the wounds of Jesus.

When someone hands you a piece of Matza bread at communion and you see the stripes and the holes, the symbolic meaning of Jesus's words "This is My body" will penetrate straight into your soul.

So why do we believe that when we dream it just simply happens? I submit to you now that dreams are symbols of what God is trying to tell you about your soul, your spirit, your life, and your purpose. He is bringing the invisible to you in pictures that you might see and believe the truths He wants you to know. You are being invisibly led and guided by mechanisms God built into man at creation in order to communicate the invisible to him. Spiritual symbols coming straight from the throne of God were woven into your DNA. You may choose to ignore them. Or you may choose to stop and give them your undivided attention. By listening to your dreams you could save yourself a wrong turn in life. Or you could discover supernaturally your destiny and your purpose.

God built healing into our bodies, and they heal themselves even though we are unaware of it. One day our flesh may be torn or damaged. In a few days it's all well, and the damage has disappeared. Our souls are the same. The soul heals itself. How does it do that? Like our flesh, it moves automatically toward health. God created it to do that.

If God is a God of symbols, and He uses the visible to show us the invisible, then it makes sense that He would use symbols in our dreams to show us the invisible pattern of perfection to which our souls are aspiring. From the fall of Man in the garden until the Resurrection of Christ we were sick in our souls, flawed, without a Savior.

But since the Resurrection we have a Savior who has lived on earth. He is our perfect pattern even though He is seated at the right hand of God in heavenly places and is invisible to us (Mark 16:19, Psalm 110:1, Hebrews 8:1, Hebrews 12:2). When we dream, and we see symbols in our dream, what is the perfect pattern that our soul is moving toward? How do we know when our soul is healed? When it reaches perfection, how do we know what perfect is? Because we have the perfect pattern…Jesus Christ, who is "the image of the invisible God, the firstborn of all creation" (Colossians 1:15).

It seems logical then that our soul is always healing itself or striving toward wholeness and healing, and we hardly realize it. It happens when we are awake and when we are sleeping. When we are sleeping, dreams are using symbols sent straight from God and His patterns in the invisible world to speak to us in order to realign our actions, our thoughts, and our feelings to make us holy and more like His Son and like Our Father.

## Warning

Unfortunately, many people choose the New Age route to understanding their dreams. They listen to and obey false teachers, horoscopes, astrologers, and others who would falsify the Word of God. Some would follow what the devil always does. He takes what is holy and powerful and makes it dirty, weak, or insignificant. Listening to New Age teachers or reading New Age books about dreams is to invite the enemy into your dream life and to give him access to your path of life. Never go there. Resist the temptation to read a New Age book about dreams. Close your eyes to reading New Age dream symbol books. They cannot possibly tell you what God is trying to make visible to you and you alone in your dreams.

## Water in dreams

When we are working on understanding our dreams and the symbols within them, it is important to first look at our own lives and ask what a symbol means to us. If the water in your dream is a river, then ask questions like, *What does a river mean to me?* Did your grandfather take you fishing on a river when you were a child? Does a river mean security in relationships? A source of food? A place to play? Merely by making associations with the symbols in our dreams a lot of times the meaning of the dream will readily come. If no association seems right, then it is important to consult the Word of God. Hopefully, you will know where the scripture is that pertains closely to your dream symbol of water. If you don't know, then look into your Bible's Concordance. There you will find a very long list of alphabetical words from the Bible and their coordinating scripture reference. It may take looking at several verses of scripture before you find one that lines up with what you feel your dream is saying. On your dream Interpretation Sheet list your symbols and their coordinating scriptures.

If you need more resources for your dream symbols, search through the biblical Cyclopedic Index in the front of your Bible. That resource will list words in alphabetical order, but it will also have meanings of words, then list the reference scripture and the page number.

The Strong's Concordance is another very useful tool for studying the scriptures. It takes every single word of the King James Version and lists where each word can be found in the scriptures. It is useful for locating scripture verses that you know the words to, but don't know the book, chapter, and verse. Also beside each verse reference there is a number. That number represents a Hebrew word (if in the Old Testament) or Greek word (if in the New Testament). In the back of the book it lists Hebrew and Greek words used to translate the Bible into English. Each has a number beside it so that you may only need to know the number to locate a Greek or Hebrew word. Then you can do a word study by reading the meaning of the original word. Whenever I refer to a number in the Strong's Concordance, you can look up the number for yourself in the Strong's Lexicon or other lexicons that use Strong's numbers to verify everything.[36] Unlike other biblical reference books, the purpose of Strong's Concordance is not to provide content or commentary about the Bible, but to provide an index to the Bible. This allows the reader to find words where they appear in the Bible. This index allows a student of the Bible to re-find a phrase or passage previously studied or to compare how the same topic is discussed in different parts of the Bible.[37]

Another helpful tool is a free Bible program called *e-sword* that can be downloaded from the Internet at www.e-sword.net. With that program you can search for any scripture, find the meaning of words, and save notes you have written to yourself.

The following chart is a list of scriptures I use when I want to look up ideas about water from the Bible. (It is not an exhaustive list):

## Symbols of Water from Scripture

| | | |
|---|---|---|
| Deliverance | Children of Israel through the Red Sea | Exodus 14:22 |
| Born again | Jesus telling Nicodemus | John 3:5 |
| Salvation (Noah Covenant (no more flood to destroy all mankind) | Noah saved through flood | 1 Peter 3:20 |
| God's own description of Himself | Telling Jeremiah about Israel | Jeremiah 2:13 |
| Peoples, Multitudes, Nations | Told by Angel | Revelation 17:15 |
| Spring of water of life-spiritual infilling | God from the throne | Revelation 21:6 |
| Water of life | Flowing from the throne in New Jerusalem | Revelation 22:1 |

| Living water | Samaritan woman | John 4:10 |
|---|---|---|
| Infilling of the Spirit | Jesus speaking at Temple during Feast of Booths | John 7:37-39 |
| Water of life without cost | The Spirit says with the bride | Revelation 22:17 |
| Sanctification | Having our hearts sprinkled clean from an evil conscience and our bodies washed with pure water | Hebrews 10: 22 |

As you work with your dreams, it is a good idea to keep a list of your own inner symbols. You will find that through the years the same symbols tend to repeat themselves.

There are unlimited resources in Holy Scripture for the symbols God has given us. Those scriptures are rich material from which to draw understanding of your dreams. There is no need to search for any other book for dream symbols. If God is speaking to you through your dreams, then the logical place to look for what God says and how He thinks is in scripture. At the back of the book I have provided charts and lists I have collected throughout the years using symbols found in scripture. They are resource materials I have collected to understand my own dreams. They should be merely a starting place for your own search through God's Word for your own symbols.

## Some Suggested Symbols That Might Work For You

I hesitate to suggest any meanings of any symbols for your dream work. But I do get asked a lot about certain symbols that show up in most people's dreams. Please, please, please do not take these as definitive dream symbols! These are only suggestions as a place for you to start if you have a dream that contain these situations.

❖❖❖❖❖

Being in public without makeup or being in public without clothes—a place to start working on this kind of dream symbol is, of course, to ask you what makeup or clothes mean to you. If you don't know where to start, start by thinking that your makeup could be a sort of mask that covers the real you. Clothes could be thought of in the same manner. Both of these things cover your public self. If you are without your public covering, then maybe you are worried that you *exposed* yourself in some situation when you were awake. Or that you will expose yourself in the future. If the other people in your dream don't seem bothered, then perhaps your exposure wasn't as big a problem as you thought it might be. If people are upset by your exposure, then maybe the dream is warning you to keep certain things to yourself. Maybe the timing is not right for your uncovering.

❖❖❖❖❖

Dreams of falling seem to be particularly troublesome to people. I recommend first of all that you, for a very short period of time, take the dream literally and check out what you fall from. The dream could be a warning dream, and it would be a shame to miss the message if your dream is telling you your stairs are unsafe or your ladder is broken. If you've checked out your accident possibilities, then consider the metaphors for falling. Are you falling in love? Are you falling from grace? Are you being demoted at work, and you think you're falling out of favor with someone? Explore what happened in your waking life for at least two or three days prior to the dream. Your unconscious could be picking up on something you haven't had time to think about. Maybe your boss is sending you mixed messages about your work, and you've been so busy you haven't paid much attention. But your unconscious is reading all the signals, and it looks like you might be falling down on the job and not realizing it.

Dreams where your teeth fall out—these dreams seem to also pertain to your public confidence in your waking life. Most of us would be embarrassed to be in a meeting and notice that our teeth are falling out. Does it mean that you can't get your teeth into the situation? Have you bitten off more than you can chew? Those are some real possibilities. If you consider the dream a warning, then have a dentist check your teeth. Your body may know something you don't know yet.

Dream tornadoes sometimes come when we are in the middle of upheaval and change in our lives. Even if they seem like nightmares, pay close attention, there is usually an answer there about how to handle the change.

Are you in a car in your dream driving down a long road? Are you driving or is someone else? Usually a car is a symbol for your vehicle through life. How do you handle life? Is your vehicle worry and fretting? Or is your vehicle peace and hopefulness? The road you are on in the dream could be your life's journey. Are you driving? Are you in control of your life? Or is someone else? Does the road remind you of a road you've been on when you were awake, and what does that road mean to you—a way to get to someone you love? Or a danger to avoid?

Dreams of flying—I had a dream one time where I was flying with no airplane, just me in the sky with my arms out to the side. It was an exhilarating experience. I was flying over hills and streams and trees. I could reach out and touch the tops of tall trees. There was no fear, just amazing wonder. If you have a flying dream, ask yourself if you are "flying high" in your waking life. Are you in line for a promotion at work? Or are you about to take a long trip in an airplane? Do you feel fearful or happy?

Dreams about sex—Everyone wants to know about sexy dreams with other people that you may or may not know. In the dream you may be enjoying sex with a neighbor or a coworker. Or you may be having sex with someone other than your spouse, and you are worried sick that they might find out. Please know that dream sex with someone does not mean that that person is interested in you in a sexual manner. Don't make that mistake! Know that the person in the dream that you are having sex with is you! Not some other person. If you are having sex with a coworker, please don't go to work the next day and pour out your heart to someone who now thinks you're an idiot.

Rather, take a deep breath and try to figure out what part of yourself you are finally loving. Is it the part of you that is creative? Or is it the part of you that is the hero? Look at the other figure in the dream, if it is someone you know, then make a short list of their qualities and figure out what about them is like you. That should give you a clue as to why some part of you is starting to love that other part. If the sex in the dream is secret or being covered up, then perhaps you should examine yourself and see if you have truly been having lustful thoughts about someone. If the answer is no, then think about the fact that you could be lusting for some part of yourself that is not giving you any attention. Is there part of you that wants a solitary vacation? Is there part of you that would love to take art lessons or a language course? You want to. You know you do. But you're afraid your family will feel betrayed or abandoned if you take time out for yourself. Your dream characters just might dress up like a hippie and try to seduce you!

Dreams about terrorists or kidnappers—Have you ever dreamed about violent situations where people from another ethnic group were chasing you? Maybe they caught you and tied you up or locked you in a closet. Or maybe you got away, narrowly escaping imprisonment. Running and running in the dream until you are exhausted, never looking back, praying someone would help. Maybe you screamed and nothing came out. You had no voice. These kinds of dreams are terrifying. It's hard to realize when these dreams happen that they are there to help you, but they are.

When thinking about the dream, be sure to examine your feelings and ideas about the ethnic group. Do your feelings come from prejudice taught to you as a child? Or did your fear of them blossom from the movies or from a scary childhood event? Examine why you are afraid of these people, who may never have done anything bad to you in your life. Then compare what you know about them to what they were doing in the dream and then to what is going on in your awake life. Are there any similarities? What is your dream saying?

If you tried to scream in the dream, and you had no voice, look at your waking life in the past few days; is there something there that you didn't get to speak your mind about? Were you forced to keep quiet in a meeting when you wanted your ideas heard? Is no one listening to you in your family or in your relationships or at church? Maybe a time will come to your mind when you know you should have spoken up but you chose to keep quiet, and you've always regretted it.

⁂

Do you dream of showing up for work or a meeting, and you are not prepared? You were supposed to bring a presentation and you forgot it. You were supposed to give a speech, and you left the speech somewhere else. You walk through the door, and a horrible feeling of inadequacy starts spreading throughout your whole body. Now what do you do? Look at your waking life. Is there some area of your life where you know deep down inside that you're not qualified to handle? Are you a new mother or a new dad? You brought the baby home from the hospital, and now the reality of being a parent has started to sink in. And you keep having these horrible dreams about not knowing what you're doing. Solve the problem by going to God in prayer. Cast all your cares upon Him because He cares for you (1 Peter 5:7 NKJV).

⁂

Someone-is-chasing-you dreams—Almost all of my life I have had dreams where someone is chasing me. I run and run and just barely stay ahead of the *bad guys*. Sometimes the running wakes me up. Sometimes they shoot me in the back, and the pain wakes me up. In my learning about dreams and the purpose of dreaming, I began to look at these dreams from a different perspective. I reasoned that if dreams are sent to heal us and not harm us, then how could these dreams be healing dreams? The answer came when I stopped asking myself why the bad guys were chasing me and began to ask myself whom I was running from. When I asked that question, answers began to come to mind.

Who or what am I running from? There was a long list to be written about that. Responsibility was on the list. Taking a leadership role at church made the list, along with learning to be a public speaker. Yes, right at the top. Sharing more of myself rather than being so extremely private. In reality there were a lot of things in my life that were chasing me. Are you the same? What is chasing you? Are you running from people, success, discipline, or pressures in life? If so, are you having chasing dreams?

Here's how I solved my problem. First I acknowledged that I had the problem, and admitted that I needed to make some changes, which I did. But pertaining to my dreams, I trained myself by telling myself that the next time someone was chasing me in a dream, I would stop running. That's right. It wasn't easy, but I did it. The next time I had a dream where someone was chasing me, I did what I always did. I ran from them as fast as I could go. But then quite suddenly, the thought came to me to stop. So I did. I stopped dead in my tracks and turned around.

I said, "What do you want?" And guess what happened? They told me. I don't remember now what it was, but it was something good. I remember that. When I woke up, I felt incredibly elated. I had faced my inner foe and found out that what they wanted was to bless me and not hurt me. From that time until now I have never had another chasing dream.

I have touched only briefly on the way God communicates to us through symbols. From the symbols in the tabernacle, the temple, and the church to untold symbols throughout His Word, God tries to turn our minds away from what the world teaches us to what He teaches us. He wants us to grasp His truths so much that He built them into our souls. When we give our souls attention we see and hear the language of our souls in our dreams.

Believe me, it takes work to learn the language our dreams speak to us. But the benefits are tremendous. They propel us exponentially ahead in our knowledge of ourselves, our purpose, and our destiny. In working on our dreams, why not ask the Author of our dreams what they mean? Who knows better than He what they mean? Who knows better what He is telling us?

In order to help with the symbols in God's Word I have created the above chart about water and other charts in the back of the book as tools for your use in understanding your dreams. They are by no means the total numbers of symbols in the Bible. But they will be helpful as a beginning place to jump start your education in the symbolic language of a God who uses symbols.

# Chapter 7: Telling Your Dreams

> O young men, if you have received a thought which dashes ahead of your times, hold to it and work at it till it comes to something. If you have dreamed a dream from the Lord, turn it over and over again till you are quite sure it is not steam from a heated brain, or smoke from hell. When it is clear to your own heart that it is fire from off God's altar—then work, and pray, and wait your time! I will now confess that, after my own fashion, I, too have seen a vision; and though you should say of me in days to come, 'Behold, this dreamer cometh,' yet, as he that hath a dream is bidden to tell his dream, so tell I mine.
>
> Charles H. Spurgeon
> Pastor and author
> Sermon given at Metropolitan Tabernacle
> April 16, 1868[38]

The sun was just beginning to peek through the curtains when the telephone rang. My husband picked up the receiver on his side of the bed. "Hello?" he asked in a sleepy mumble.

A voice answered on the other end, "Is Gloria awake yet? I've got to ask her about a dream!"

Bill tossed the phone to me saying, "It's for you. It's about a dream."

The phone was caught in one hand while my other one searched on the floor for my clipboard and pen. "Hello," I said into the receiver, trying to focus my eyes.

Frequently the morning begins with a telephone call from someone who has had a *significant* dream they just have to tell someone. They think they need help quickly, before they forget what they dreamed. My first question is, "Did you write it down?"

More times than not, the answer is "No, not yet. I wanted to talk to you first."

People who know me well know that this response elicits a tiny sigh. They know that I say repeatedly, "If you don't write it down in the first ten minutes after waking, you'll lose a lot of details. After you've written it down, *then* let's talk."

The problem with telling your dream before you write it down is that 1) you've already forgotten many details and 2) there is a danger that after you know what it means you'll be on your merry way, and you may never write it down. If you never write it down, you may miss the bigger picture of what God is trying to tell you. Perhaps that one dream is only a small part of a dream series where God is revealing future plans for you—one dream at a time.

## The Benefits of Sharing Your Dreams

Any time we share our thoughts, ideas, or feelings with other people we get a new perspective. What seemed to be one way in our minds sometimes turns out to be something different as we talk about it. Another person may see what we think is a burden as a blessing in disguise. Or a solution to a problem may be evident to someone else, when we can't see it at all.

When it comes to our dreams, we may need another's point of view in order to see what is right before our eyes—our mental and spiritual eyes, that is. Someone else, whether they realize it or not, may innocently ask the exact question that will jog our mental pictures, to reveal a true symbol previously hidden to us.

In telling our dream to a fellow Christian or what I call a *holy friend,* the dream becomes even more printed on our souls than if we simply think about it. The more times you interact with a dream, the more permanent it becomes in your memory and in your Spirit. In other words, if you write the dream down, and tell the dream, the less likely you are to ever forget it.

Remembering your dreams makes your life richer, fuller, and deeper. You become aware of a deeper level in your soul and your spirit, and you become aware that God really does love you and wants to communicate with you. As you become sensitive to your dream language and its voice, you also become more sensitive to God's voice. One friend calls it "learning the deeper things of God."

Sharing your dreams with someone is a great way to impose accountability on yourself if you have a problem with self-discipline. Knowing that you will be asked about your dreams on a regular basis by a trusted friend might be just the nudge you need to begin keeping a dream journal.

If you choose to tell your dreams to a holy friend or spiritual director on a regular basis, soon you will be enthusiastic about the time you set aside for this interior work. It becomes a sacred time that you won't want to miss. The time venturing inward becomes rich with expectation and desire for revelation knowledge—a walk out of darkness into the light.

The telling of your dreams, especially those that might provoke fear or anxiety, seems to bring balance and peace into the strong emotions sometimes evoked by such dreams. In hearing our own voice relate the feelings aloud, bigger-than-life dreams shrink in our minds to proper significance. A holy friend can help you *walk through* a dream and see the symbols for what they really mean by asking the right questions, which engage your mind instead of your emotions in the *figuring out* process of dreamwork.

Working with a holy friend to interpret our dreams brings our spirit into community with another person's spirit, and Jesus says, "For where two or three have gathered together in My name, there I am in their midst" (Matthew 18:20). When your spirit and another's spirit are working together to understand what God is saying to you, it becomes an invitation for Jesus to be present—a holy endeavor. When this happens, understanding and revelation begin, and things you didn't know previously about yourself become infinitely clearer.

Opening yourself to another person through prayerful dream work has many side benefits that are almost separate from the dream work itself. In baring ourselves to a trusted friend through the telling of our dreams, trust grows with the practice of it. Soon pride begins to diminish as we admit to ourselves that God loves us so much that He tries to communicate with us on a regular basis, whether we always listen or not. And soon our hearts open like previously closed flowers to receive all the love that God wants to pour out on us.

By telling our dreams to a holy friend or other person, we also listen to their dreams and feelings. In the context of the shared experience both are supported and encouraged in the Lord. The Holy Spirit in each of us reaches out to enrich the spiritual life of the other. It is comforting to learn that what is happening to you is also happening to someone else. Learning that your dreams are not *weird* or *bizarre*, but very ordinary and normal, is a very comforting feeling. It is helpful to validate another person's dream life and have yours validated in return.

A holy friend shared with me that she "can now see that my dreams are pretty normal, except that I know God tailor-made mine especially for me. Imagine that." And "it wasn't until I started telling my dreams to a special friend that I discovered they weren't scary at all, but were trying to tell me something I had always refused to hear."

Would you like to share your dreams with someone? Who would you choose? A pastor? A family member? A friend? Who can you trust with your dreams?

## Whom Do You Tell?

Telling someone else your dreams is, for a woman, similar to letting someone see her without her makeup. It's a scary thing at first. After all, you'll have to reveal things about yourself that no one else knows. Dealing with dreams is like peeling the layers of an onion. Layer after layer comes off until there are no layers left, but with each layer a rich aroma is released.

Choosing the right person to help you peel the layers away is sometimes a delicate situation. Should it be your best friend who already knows *all* your secrets? Or should it be your husband or wife with whom you feel safe? Maybe your pastor would be best? But does the pastor know anything about dreams? Or even believe they are useful?

First and foremost, the person you share your dreams with should be a Christian who, of course, believes in God, Jesus, and the Holy Spirit. If that Christian belief system is in place, then the foundation for your Christian dream work will be built on solid ground.

You should also choose a person who is respectful of things of the soul. He or she should have a reverential attitude toward you and your spiritual journey. In their hearts, they should keep the proper perspective about dreams, that is, *not* wander away from believing that dreams come from God.

It almost goes without saying that the person you share your dreams with should be likable, easy to work with, and realistically compatible with you. You should be able to trust them with your innermost thoughts and feelings. They should be a person whom you can keep as a confidant.

It would be helpful if they already know something about dreams. At the very least, they should be someone who remembers their own dreams. Working with dreams takes a certain amount of creativity and imagination. So the person you share your dreams with should be a person who can visualize what your dream looks like and how it might have had the effect on you it had.

It is also essential that when you choose your partner for dream work that you look for a person who really listens to you. That might mean that your partner should have enough time set aside to work with you and not be so busy that they are distracted from the work at hand. Whether your time together is long or short, it should be looked on as a special time not to be taken for granted or easily upstaged by interruptions.

You both might find it beneficial to schedule your time together at the same place, the same day, and the same time each time you meet in order to create a symbol for yourselves that says, "Our dream work time is holy time or holy ground." Or, "this is the time that we will make ourselves available to the Holy Spirit so that answers will come about our dreams."

Not only should your dream partner be a good listener, but he/she should also know when to speak and what to say. They should know when to ask questions and when to give encouragement. When you are on the right track of discovering the true meaning of your dream, good encouragement would be statements like:

"Yes, I think you're right," or, "That sounds right to me," and, "Yes, I think you're getting the right idea."

Sometimes a dream partner needs to give you comfort. When the layers are being peeled away, as I talked about before, deep feelings and emotions become exposed. When this happens, it's good to have a fellow traveler to give you a hug and gently encourage you to venture forth into new interior territory.

It is also very helpful if you and your dream partner have a good grasp of Holy Scripture. The better you know the Bible, the better you can discern what God is trying to tell you in your dreams. Often the answer to your dreams is as close as your Bible. But where do you look for answers if you aren't familiar with the book? Take the time each day to read scripture. It will be most helpful in finding sound and sensible meanings to your dreams.

You should practice taking a word or a symbol from a dream and looking that word up in the Concordance of your Bible. Knowing what God's Word says about an aspect of your life could make all the difference in the world when it comes to understanding your dream. Very often finding the right scripture that coincides with a dream makes the words seem to jump off the page at you. Or, some people say, "It blew me away!" That is how powerful the connection is between the kingdom within us, God's Holy Spirit, and God's words from scripture.

The Bible itself tells us about that power. It says, "The word of God is living and active and sharper than any two-edged sword, and piercing as far as the division of soul and spirit, of both joints and marrow, and able to judge the thoughts and intentions of the heart" (Hebrews 4:12). That power comes through loud and clear when we are able to connect it with our minds and hearts, our very souls, and the messages it sends in our sleep.

You may find a clear explanation for one of your dream symbols in Revelation or in Daniel or in any other book of scripture. It helps tremendously in dream work if you know what's in the Bible and how it's organized, so you can simply turn to the page where the answer might be located. Joseph said about dreams that "…interpretations belong to God" (Genesis 40:8). Since that is true, then where better to find the answer to your dream interpretation than in God's book!

If you'll recall in Genesis 37:5-20 Joseph chose to tell his two dreams to his brothers, who turned out to be bad choices of people with whom to share his dreams. When Joseph told them his dreams, they did not encourage him. They did not comfort him. They were not respectful of his spiritual journey. Instead, they became jealous! They jeered at him saying, "Here comes this dreamer!" Later they even plotted to kill him (Genesis 37:19).

That illustration shows how important it is to choose wisely when sharing your dreams. In some cases your family members might not be the best persons with whom to share your dreams. Not unless they meet most of the requirements I've previously discussed. You might even want to share your dreams with someone you hardly know personally, such as clergy from a different church, or a nun, or a monk. It is still important, however, that they respect the place dreams play in individuals, communities, and the Body of Christ.

Unfortunately, there are clergy in the church today who ignore or denounce interior work, and therefore have no interest whatsoever in dreams. If you encounter such an attitude, thank them kindly for their time and move on until you meet a man or woman of God who appreciates the work of the Holy Spirit revealed through dreams.

Morton Kelsey addresses this situation in his book, *God, Dreams & Revelation* and encourages a change of attitude, when he states:

> The church at the present is saddled with the prejudice of modern culture that only the material and the rational are real and significant. Consideration of the dream will help us break out of this prejudice and realize that there is another realm of being, a realm in which the ancient church was a specialist, as the modern church needs to be now.[39]

## What a Dream Partner Should and Shouldn't Say

When you and the person you've chosen to tell your dreams to are together and ready to begin looking at a dream, in order to keep the proper perspective, it is important to begin with a prayer. Be sure to thank God for creating dreams and for speaking to us through them. Thank Jesus for being in your meeting because the two of you are gathered in His name. Invite the Holy Spirit to be present and to reveal unknown truths to the both of you.

Begin by working on one dream at a time. Tell your dream or read it from what you've written in your dream journal. Show your dream partner any drawings you may have done. Discuss the feelings you had during the dream and immediately following. Discuss what is going on in your life at the present time that might relate to your dream.

The person hearing your dream should only listen while you are telling your dream, not only noticing what you say, but also how you say it. They should notice how animated you are so they will pick up hints of how the dream affected you. This is the time for *active* listening.

As you tell your dream, the listener should feel free to ask clarifying questions, so that they understand what happened in the dream, as long as these are short questions and let you keep talking. Taking notes during this time would be advisable in order to remember details for later.

What the listener should not do is immediately tell you what they think your dream means after you are finished talking…unless your dream partner has a particular gift of interpreting dreams! The best thing is for the dream partner to begin asking questions that might encourage the dreamer to explore his/her feelings about the dream. Such as: "Did you feel frightened in the dream?" or, "Were you depressed?" or, "Were you happy?"

Remember: the most likely person to know what the dream means is the dreamer herself. The dream partner should ask questions and make suggestions, but never insist that they have all the answers to the meaning of the dream…unless they have had a revelation from God about the meaning of the dream. If the dreamer has properly interpreted the dream, he/she will say so. The *Aha!* response will automatically spill out. If the dream partner disagrees, it is not a good idea to dispute what the dreamer believes is the real meaning of the dream. After all, the dream was given to the dreamer not to the dream partner. But if the dreamer is obviously wrong, keep asking questions until the truth becomes clear.

The goal in telling your dream to someone else is always to discover the true meaning of the dream. When the cupbearer and the baker were in jail with Joseph, they both had a dream on the same night. Like all dreams, each dream had its own meaning or interpretation. They both felt dejected and sad about their dreams, and they knew they needed someone to talk to about them. In this instance, they couldn't figure out their dreams on their own.

They said to Joseph when he noticed their sadness, "We have had a dream, and there is no one to interpret it."

Joseph answered them, and said, "Do not interpretations belong to God? Tell it to me, please" (Genesis 40:8). He had confidence that God would reveal the meaning of the dreams to him.

Joseph spoke up immediately after hearing each dream and told the interpretation of the dream. And the accuracy of his interpretations proved to be true. Therefore, we can assume that Joseph had a gift for interpreting dreams or he was given a revelation from God as to the meaning. Most people do not have that gift. Most people have to work on their dreams by putting their *figuring out* skills to work.

Even if neither you nor your partner has the gift of interpreting dreams, it is still very possible for one or both of you to figure out what your dream is saying. What is sought after is truth. What is God *really* trying to tell you?

## Telling Your Dreams In a Group

Once I attended a Christian seminar, and one of the ice breakers used to get people talking was to ask those who were introverts to stand on one side of the room and the extroverts to stand on the other side. There was a great shuffling around as the group of one hundred people divided up. A few giggled. A few looked at their feet. But in a little while there were definitely two distinct groups. What was interesting, however, was *how* the groups were standing. The extroverts were all huddled closely together and were talking and laughing. Across the room the introverts were standing separated, not touching and not talking. Many had their arms folded. Some still stared at their feet.

The moral of the story is: we're not all alike. Some are social. Some are not. Some of us love a group. It energizes us. We get ideas. Our brains seem to go into overdrive. We figure things out better when we have multiple sources of input—the more the better. On the other hand, there are some of us who would almost rather die than sit in a group. We can't think clearly when there are other people around. We love solitude. We get our best ideas when we're alone.

What kind of person are you? Do you crave other people's opinions? Or had you rather figure yourself out without anyone's input?

Integrate these suggestions into your dream work analyses. They might help you in turning on the light.

1. Practice listening. Practice asking and offering explanations.

2. Watch to see which thought clicks, both in the person's mind and in his life, and also which interpretations misfire.

3. As you meet for this interior work, you'll come to know a great deal about the other person, about her conscious life, and her convictions. As you become familiar with her life, the dreams will make sense against the backdrop of a whole life.

4. Listen to your own dreams in order to help other people understand theirs. It's easier to recognize the divine significance in dreams if you already know God. You must be open to the voice of God and be able to recognize Him.

5. It would help if you know the religious traditions of mankind in order to know how to bring life to the symbols in dreams and amplify their meaning.

6. Treat every dream with respect. It is a message from your soul sent to heal you and make you whole.

## Never Chase After a Dream Partner

If you want a friend to share your dreams with, pray. Then wait patiently on the Lord. God will hear your prayer and send you someone—more than likely that someone will be better than anyone you could have tracked down and begged to be your partner.

I never seek a dream partner. I let my desires be known to God. Then I wait and watch. I actively listen, having ears to hear. If I get a hint of someone, I approach them in private and ask if they listen to their dreams. If they don't, I move on, waiting once again.

One of the dangers of chasing after a dream partner is that you might catch someone who is definitely the wrong partner, but they will agree to help you for all the wrong reasons. Maybe they have a hidden agenda. Maybe they don't listen to their dreams and don't want to. Maybe they just couldn't say no to you. The dream partner that God sends is always better than the one we track down and capture because we couldn't wait on Him.

## Beware of False Prophets

Be very careful with whom you share your dreams. Not everyone respects the things of the soul. Not everyone is where you are on your spiritual journey. There are those people, some of them Christians, who will trample on your dreams. Their motives might be wanting to help or trying to give advice, but they might have unconscious damaging motives also. They might be jealous of your new growth. They might be envious of your closeness to God. May you use your best discernment in choosing a dream partner.

If the person you shared your dreams with says, "I know exactly what your dream means, and here's what you should do about it." Thank them kindly and run. Rather, watch for a listener, someone with wisdom, and someone who will speak the Word of God to you about your dreams.

Those who have your dreams all figured out do not have your best interests at heart. Pride and arrogance may have overtaken them, and they only want a pat on the back for being so prophetic about you and your life. Beware that they want to lead you away from God and toward themselves.

Your dream partner or spiritual director should always point you in the direction of the Lord. It should never be about them. It should always be about you and helping you to hear from God. Always test the word of a dream partner or spiritual director against the Word of God to see if it is the truth.

God said, "Is there anything in the hearts of the prophets who prophesy falsehood…who intend to make My people forget My name by their dreams which they relate to one another…" (Jeremiah 23:26-27). Test in your heart what the dream partner or spiritual director is telling you. Does it point to God? Does it line up with the truth of God's Word? Does it help me hear God better? Or is this leading away from God? Am I forgetting God's name in this relationship?

If the relationship becomes something other than hearing God's voice, then leave it. Sever the relationship and move on. Go find yourself another dream partner, another spiritual director. Do not let much time pass. This work is too important to waste any time on results that are false.

In Jeremiah 23:30-32, God says, "…I am against the prophets who steal My words from each other. Behold, I am against the prophets who use their tongues and declare, '*The Lord* declares.' Behold, I am against those who prophesied false dreams…" Take these words seriously. Test what anyone tells you about your dreams. Remember that you are the only person who really knows what your dreams mean. Find a dream partner or spiritual director who will help you find God's truth.

Especially beware of books that claim to know all the answers about what dream symbols mean. Many books will tell you what a snake means, what a house means, what danger means. Unfortunately, those books are usually not Christian books. So avoid them. Symbols do not always mean the same thing for different people. Who knows the mind and heart of another?

Only God does. Listen to what your soul and spirit are telling you about a symbol in your dream. Do not listen to books written by false prophets. "They speak a vision of their own imagination" (Jeremiah 23:16).

Please understand that there are prophets who are not sent by God. There are authors of dream books who have not been taught by God about dreams. They research science, New Age authors, and write books. God did not send them to do that work. God did not speak to them about what they wrote. They ran without being sent. They prophesied without God speaking to them.

Interior work is holy work. Your spirit and soul are involved. It is precious to God. Do not trust the fruit of your spirit and soul to those who would treat it as nothing. Be a good steward of dreams, as if they were each a precious gift from God, because they are. They are multi-level treasures which unfold and keep unfolding to reveal hidden mysteries of your most private thoughts and feelings.

What happened to King Belshazzar, king of Babylon, when he treated God's precious vessels as if they were lowly and common things? As you'll recall, the king was having a party, and in the middle of the party he had the idea that he would impress his guests by bringing in the gold and silver vessels that his father stole from the temple in Jerusalem. He thought his friends might have some fun drinking their wine out of golden goblets. He had no regard for the precious things of God. He put no confidence in the vessels from God's house in the holy city.

But God didn't take this affront lightly. Suddenly the king was seeing an invisible man's hand writing a message from God on the wall, and it frightened him so badly that his knees were knocking! Was praising the gods of gold and silver while drinking from God's holy vessels worth this much terror? Not only was the messenger frightening, but so also was the message. The message on the wall told King Belshazzar that his kingdom was over. It was just a matter of time (Daniel 6:25-28). This should be a lesson to those of us who have the responsibility of handling dreams. It is vitally important to remember that they are God's messages, not something to play around with.

Even the prophet Daniel, when he was brought before King Nebuchadnezzar to tell him the King's dream and its interpretation, knew it wasn't about him. He knew it was about the King and his relationship with God. He and his friends had already prayed about the King's dream, and God had answered the prayer. When Daniel was brought face-to-face with Nebuchadnezzar, he pointed the King to God, not to himself.

Nebuchadnezzar asked Daniel whether he was able to tell him his dream and its interpretation. And Daniel answered that there was no one able to tell him what he wanted to know. He went on to say, "However, there is a God in heaven who reveals mysteries, and He has made known to King Nebuchadnezzar what will take place in the latter days" (Daniel 2:28). Daniel wanted the King to know that God was the center of that situation, not Daniel. Remember that when you work on dreams with a partner.

In their conversation, Daniel never prided himself in being the King's dream interpreter. In fact he humbled himself and kept confirming that the dream was about God and His relationship with King Nebuchadnezzar. This is the job of the dream partner or spiritual director, to keep in mind that her job is to help the dreamer connect with the Giver of dreams.

Daniel said, "But as for me, this mystery has not been revealed to me for any wisdom residing in me more than in any other living man, but for the purpose of making the interpretation known to the king, and that you may understand the thoughts of your mind" (Daniel 2:30). This is a prime example of the humble attitude a spiritual director should have. They should know that they don't have all the answers. They should be looking to God for the answers. They should be praying over you and your dreams. The dream partner or spiritual director should know their purpose. To help you understand what God is trying to tell you. If that is not what is happening with you, find another spiritual director.

If there is any doubt left in you about having a Godly dream partner or spiritual director, consider this. In Deuteronomy, God told the children of Israel to listen to His voice, serve Him, and cling to Him. But if a prophet or a *dreamer of dreams* should "counsel rebellion against the Lord your God who brought you from the land of Egypt and redeemed you from the house of slavery, to seduce you from the way in which the Lord your God commanded you to walk. So you shall purge the evil from among you." The Bible says that the prophet or *dreamer of dreams* who rebels against God shall be put to death (Deuteronomy 13:1-5).

Listen to God's Word. If a dream partner or spiritual director should ever counsel you to disobey God, not to listen to God's voice, or to rebel against God or His gospel in any way, reject that counsel and leave. It doesn't matter if their feelings get hurt. It doesn't matter if they get angry with you. It doesn't matter if they never speak to you again. It only matters that you obey God and His Word.

## Benefits Are Everlasting Riches

God loves you so much He will use anything to save you, to heal you, and to bring you to Him so that you may live with Him forever. He'll speak to you through billboards, through bumper stickers, through music, sermons, and dreams. Understanding just one significant dream can take you to a *high* you've never known before and leave you there for weeks, months, or years. Why? Because it is *solid evidence* that you've connected with a real God who cares about you.

The benefits of understanding your dreams start immediately. Then they continue to unfold, grow, and multiply. It is not a phenomenon for only the young either. Old men (and women) have dreams. God speaks to everyone through their dreams. Does everyone hear Him speaking? Unfortunately, no, but for those who have the courage to take the trip, it is full of treasure beyond measure. Pearls of wisdom float to the top of your conscious mind. Priceless gems that last forever are yours, if you will only take the time to search them out.

Are you bored with watching television? Why not watch the theater of your mind? If you are willing to watch and listen, God will unfold to you hidden mysteries of the kingdom that is within you. Riches await—great and mighty things, which you do not know (Jeremiah 33:3), are waiting in your dreams to be revealed and understood.

# Chapter 8: Famous Christians' Dreams

> Hear now My words: If there is a prophet among you, I, the Lord, shall make Myself known to him in a vision. I shall speak with him in a dream.
>
> God speaking to Aaron and Miriam
> Numbers 12:6

As Christians we are all familiar with the fact that Jesus's life began with dreams and angels. (Matthew 1:20, 24, 2:12-14, 19-22 and Luke 1:11, 13, 18, 19, 26, 30, 34, 2:9-10, 2:13) Take heart. God is still speaking to people through their dreams. It doesn't matter if you are famous or obscure. It makes no difference if you are rich or poor. What matters is that you interpret your dreams and do what God tells you to do, if anything. Do you understand your dreams as coming from God or not? That alone is what makes the difference between your dreams only being *that thing your brain does* or whether your dreams are an avenue to intensify your relationship with the living God.

## St. Francis's Dream

Such a person is St. Francis of Assisi. You may associate him with the Roman Catholic Church or with being the monk who preached to birds and animals or with being the author of the St. Francis Prayer. Many people love his prayer that says:

> Lord, make us instruments of your peace. Where there is hatred, let us sow love; where there is injury, pardon; where there is discord, union; where there is doubt, faith; where there is despair, hope; where there is darkness, light; where there is sadness, joy. Grant that we may not so much seek to be consoled as to console; to be understood as to understand; to be loved as to love. For it is in giving that we receive; it is in pardoning that we are pardoned; and it is in dying that we are born to eternal life. Amen.[40]

Few people know that a dream played a significant role in the conversion of St. Francis. When Francis was just barely twenty years old, he fought in the war between Assisi and Perugia and was taken prisoner. A low fever that he contracted appears to have turned his thoughts to the things of eternity. The weaker his body became, the more deeply his sense of charity and love toward others took root in him. By the time he returned to Assisi he was seriously ill. His mother's care for him brought him back to health, but the carefree life he had led before his captivity seemed empty to him. Driven by his desire to be a soldier, he decided to follow a knight of Assisi to the southern region of Apulia, but when he had gotten as far as Spoleto, the Lord appeared to him one night in a dream and ordered him to turn back. The words of God echoed in his mind like a summons, and he obeyed the Lord. This marked the beginning of his gradual conversion and from that moment on, his life was to be filled with prophetic events. That dream greatly intensified Francis's relationship with the living God. The year was 1250. Two years after his death in 1226 he was canonized by the Roman Catholic Church as a saint.[41]

## John Bosco's Dreams

In the Roman Catholic Church there is an organization called Salesian Missions that helps poor children in over 125 countries around the world. The famous Bishop Fulton Sheen once called them a "modern miracle."[42] From humble beginnings in the last century, the Salesians of John Bosco have become one of three largest religious families of men and women in the Catholic Church worldwide. And it all began with a dream.

When John Bosco was a boy of nine years old he dreamed he was in a field with a crowd of children. Those children started cursing and misbehaving, and John jumped into the crowd to try to stop them. In order to stop them he, too, became angry and began to fight. Suddenly a man with a face filled with light appeared, dressed in a white flowing mantle. The man called John over and made him leader of the boys. John was stunned at being put in charge of the unruly gang.

The man said to him, "You will have to win these friends of yours not with blows but with gentleness and kindness."

John answered, "I'm just a boy. How can you order me to do something that looks impossible?"

The man answered, "What seems so impossible you must achieve by being obedient and acquiring knowledge."

Then the boys turned into the wild animals they had been acting like. The man told John that this was the field of John's life work. Once John changed and grew in humility, faithfulness, and strength, he would see a change in the children. The wild animals suddenly turned into gentle lambs.[43]

Like Joseph in the Bible, John Bosco shared his dreams with his family and his brothers laughed at him. Even when he told his grandmother, she said, "You mustn't pay any attention to dreams."

But John replied, "I felt the same way about it, yet I could never get that dream out of my head." Eventually that first dream led him to minister to poor and neglected boys. He learned how to relate to young boys, how to entertain them in order to win their trust, and then how to minister to them when they came to him for help. Once he had their attention with his juggling and with games, he would teach them and take them to church. Often John acted on his dreams simply by sharing them, sometimes repeating them to several different individuals or groups he thought would be affected by his dreams.

The groups of boys he worked with and helped received the most benefit from John's dreams. Their lives were changed and improved drastically because of John's dreams and his obedience in remembering his dreams and using them in his ministry to poor children. For example, he used several dreams to remind the boys to keep to a good and moral life. In one dream he saw the boys eating bread of four kinds—tasty rolls, ordinary bread, coarse bread, and moldy bread, which represented the state of the boys' souls. He said he would be glad to talk to any boys who wanted to know which bread they were eating and then proceeded to use the occasion to give them moral guidance. Through his dreams John Bosco created the Salesian Missions, which continues on with his work today around the world.[44]

## Ronald Reagan's Recurring Dream

Ever since his childhood, Ronald Reagan had had a recurring dream. Though he had lived in numerous homes in his lifetime he had always dreamed that he was living in a big white house. The dream "just kept coming back," he told his speech writer, Peggy Noonan. "And it was that I was going to live in a sort of mansion with big rooms like this one–high ceilings, white walls. And I'd have it over and over." After he became president of the United States and moved into the White House, the dreams stopped for good.[45]

## Warning Dream for Ronald Reagan

Joan Sieffert, president of the Pittsburgh chapter of actor Ronald Reagan's fan club, exchanged letters with Reagan well into the 1970s. One night in 1974, Sieffert awoke from a dream in which she pictured Reagan running for president, winning, and then being shot. "He was shot before entering a car," she said, "and it really terrified me." The next morning she sent off a letter to the Reagans informing them of her dream. A few days later Joan received a telephone call from Nancy Reagan telling her she feared something like this could happen someday, and so did her husband. Seven years later on March 30, 1981 while President Reagan was leaving the Washington Hilton after giving a speech, a young man named John Hinckley shot him in order to impress the actress Jodie Foster. Joan Sieffert's warning dream had actually happened.[46]

## Betty Robison's Dream

The popular evangelist, James Robison, relates the details of a dream that his wife, Betty, experienced in his book, *Free At Last!* He tells that their daughter, Robin, had a blister-type growth on her lip that kept growing for several weeks. It was painful and unsightly, and they began to pray about it and also see doctors. After three months, the blister was the size of a marble and Betty went into intercessory prayer for Robin. Then Betty had a dream.

Betty says:

> I went to bed that night weeping and praying for her. I dreamed that Robin put her hand up to her lip and that the growth fell off in her hand. When I awoke, I ran into her room, fully expecting it to be gone, but it wasn't. My heart was broken.
>
> I told her about my dream, and later that day she admitted that she was rehearsing her testimony

> for when God removed the sore. I pleaded with the Lord to honor her faith and not to let her be disappointed. That night, Dudley Hall and his family prayed for Robin because they thought the sore looked more painful than ever. Before James left for a trip, we agreed in prayer that the thing would *be gone by that Thursday.*[47]

James says in the book that on Thursday, at four o'clock in the morning, Robin came running into Betty's room and woke her up, so excited, yelling, 'Mother! Mother! Look! Look!"

Just as in Betty's dream, the sore had fallen off in Robin's hand.

Healing, instruction, revelation, and more are available through listening to one's dreams. If one-third of our lives is spent sleeping and much of that is spent dreaming, then it only makes sense that by awakening to your dream life, you'll be awakening to one-third of your life that you know nothing about at the present time! Jesus says that He has come that you might have life, and that you might have it abundantly (John 10:10). There is an abundant world inside each of us that is just waiting for us to discover it. When we do, it rewards us with never-before-found treasures and truths.

## John A. Sanford's Father's Dream

John A. Sanford, an Episcopal priest and author of *Dreams: God's Forgotten Language*, wrote an interesting account of a dream his father had a week before he died. Like John, his father was a priest and so was his father. Immediately upon having the dream he told it to his wife, and she wrote it down:

> In the dream he awakened in his living room. But then the room changed and he was back in his room in the old house in Vermont as a child. Again the room changed: to Connecticut (where he had his first job), to China, to Pennsylvania (where he often visited), to New Jersey, and then back to the living room. In each scene after China, I (John's mother) was present, in each instance being of a different age in accordance with the time represented. Finally he sees himself lying on the couch back in the living room. I am descending the stairs and the doctor is in the room. The doctor says, 'Oh, he's gone.' Then, as the others fade in the dream, he sees the clock on the mantelpiece, the hands have been moving, but now they stop, as they stop, a window opens behind the mantelpiece clock and a bright light shines through. The opening widens into a door and the light becomes a brilliant path. He walks out on the path of light and disappears.[48]

John Sanford talks in his book about how comforting this dream was to his father and that he no longer had any anxiety about his death after the dream. He also says that they used the dream as inspiration for his father's grave marker, which says *the path of light* down which he went.[49]

# Jarena Lee's Dream

It couldn't have been easy for an African-American woman in the 1800s to follow her calling. But that is exactly what Jarena Lee did. In 1819, Jarena Lee became the first woman to be authorized to preach by Richard Allen, founder of the African Methodist Episcopal Church. Even though she was authorized by the church, she still faced obstacles and hostility as she traveled across the country spreading the good news of Jesus Christ. In one year alone, she traveled 2,325 miles on foot and preached 178 sermons. Jarena Lee was a woman who listened to her dreams.

In 1811, Jarena married a man named Joseph Lee, pastor of a Society at Snow Hill, about six miles outside of Philadelphia. After she and Joseph had lived in Snow Hill for about a year, Jarena was discontented and began to appeal to her husband for them to move into the city of Philadelphia. But Joseph was not inclined to leave his congregation. One night Jarena had a dream that she believed showed her God's will concerning the matter:

> I dreamed that as I was walking on the summit of a beautiful hill, that I saw near me a flock of sheep, fair and white, as if but newly washed; when there came walking toward me a man of a grave and dignified countenance, dressed entirely in white, as it were a robe, and looking at me, said emphatically, 'Joseph Lee must take care of these sheep, or the wolf will come and devour them.' When I awoke I was convinced of my error, and immediately, with a glad heart,

> yielded to the right spirit in the Lord. This also greatly strengthened my faith in his care over them, for fear the wolf should by some means take any of them away.[50]

Some time later Jarena became very sick, so sick that she could not sit up. According to her journal she "did not expect to recover" from her illness. In spite of her ill health, she earnestly prayed that the Lord would heal her and raise her up. Shortly after, she had another dream:

> I thought I saw the sun rise in the morning, and ascend to an altitude of about half an hour high, and then become obscured by a dense black cloud, which continued to hide its rays for about one-third part of the day, and then it burst forth again with renewed splendor.[51]

She interpreted her dream to signify that her early life—her conversion to God—was the sunrise in the morning, that her sickness was the dense black cloud, and that the bursting forth of the sun again was the recovery of her health. This dream and its message sent her to her knees where she prayed, and she believed that the Lord answered by saying to her heart, "You shall be restored to your health again and worship God in full purpose of heart."

After Jarena's husband died only six years into their marriage, she was left alone with two infant children, but despite many hardships she continued on with her preaching ministry. Armed with the full knowledge that the Lord was at her side, she pressed forward. In 1833 she began working with an editor to turn her religious journal into an autobiography. Three years later she had one thousand copies printed and began distributing it at camp meetings and on the street. By 1849, only twelve years before the Civil War, she printed an expanded version that became her autobiography.

## Rodney Howard-Browne's Dream

The charismatic evangelist, Rodney Howard-Browne, also listens to his dreams. Howard-Browne is the South African evangelist who started the *Laughing Revival* in 1993 which led eventually to the *Toronto Blessing* in Ontario and the *Pensacola Outpouring* in Pensacola, Florida. In fact a dream is what led him to plan his massive crusade in New York City in 1999. The following dream was described by Rodney Howard-Browne:

> I had a dream in which Billy Graham was talking to me about his crusade in New York in 1957. A crusade that lasted 3 1/2 months, 2,000,000 people came through the doors of Madison Square Garden, and 55,000 people were saved. As I listened to Billy Graham speak in my dream, my heart just broke for New York City, and I started weeping. I wept so hard that when I woke up, my pillow was soaked with tears. As I got out of bed, I knew we had to go to New York and launch one of the biggest soul winning crusades since 1957. It just dropped in my spirit and I knew it by the Holy Ghost.[52]

Reassured by the dream, Howard-Browne made plans for his own crusade. He rented Madison Square Garden for what started out to be a six-week crusade and went for three and a half months. During this time in New York, two million people attended the meeting at the Garden and 55,000 decisions were made for Christ. The crusade, called Good News New York, ran from July 7 to August 14, 1999.

## Constantine's Dream

The Roman emperor Constantine had a dream that confirmed a vision. He was in a war against his brother-in-law and co-emperor, Maxentius. According to Eusebius, the historian, Constantine was convinced that he needed divine assistance from God before a crucial battle of Milvian Bridge.[53] While Constantine was praying for such assistance, God sent him a vision of a cross of light at midday, bearing the inscription *In hoc signo vinces* (meaning: in this sign you will be victorious).

That night he had a dream that reaffirmed his earlier vision. God told Constantine to use the sign he had been given as a safeguard in all of his battles. Thus, Constantine converted to Christianity and ordered the symbol of his Savior's name (the intersection of the Greek letter *chi* and *rho*) to represent his army. Constantine was victorious in the battle of the Milvian Bridge, and he continued to wear the symbol for Christ against every hostile power he faced.[54]

God is the same yesterday, today, and forever. If God spoke to people in the Bible through dreams and He spoke to people in the Middle Ages through dreams, why won't He speak to you today through your dreams? He most certainly will. Slow down, quiet yourself, and write down what God is saying to you in your dreams. With practice you will soon learn what He is saying.

## Bill Johnson's Dream

In Bill Johnson's book, *Dreaming With God*, he relates two dreams that are important to his ministry:

> As I was preparing to come to Bethel Church to be their new pastor, I had a dream warning me of the potential danger in the coming transition. In the dream I was taking an exit off of a freeway. I was then to cross over the roadway on an overpass, and get back on the freeway going in the opposite direction. When doing so I noticed that the road was icy and that I would need to be cautious as to how fast I made the turn or I would roll my vehicle off the embankment back onto the freeway. I woke up and realized that God just warned me not to make the needed changes too quickly. While some might have felt our transition happened rather fast, it was much slower than it would have been without that dream. Each step was preceded by a clear word from God.
>
> He let me know when that season of "cautious turning" was over through another dream. In it I saw the same freeway, but this time I was going the opposite direction. There was bright green grass on both sides of the road, and the pave-

> ment was wet from the melted ice. As strange as it may sound, the water didn't pose any danger to traveling at high speeds but instead was a sign of His fresh outpouring. The ice, that made a quick transition dangerous and unwise, had melted. There were no other cars to slow down or impede our progress. In giving me this dream He spoke, saying, "It's time to pull out the stops." This second dream occurred around 18 months after the first one. The majority of the people had left that were going to leave and I was now given liberty to go at a pace more suitable to the increasing winds of change.[55]

## Kenneth E. Hagin's Dream

In Kenneth E. Hagin's book *The Believer's Authority*, he relates an important dream in his life that taught him a lesson about the power of standing your ground and being strong in the Lord. Hagin told his dream this way:

> In 1942, while pastoring in east Texas, I had a test in my body. I didn't tell anyone about it except the Lord. I prayed and believed He would heal me. Then I stood my ground.
>
> In the nighttime I would be awakened with alarming heart symptoms, and I would get up and pray. I battled that thing for about six weeks. One night I had great difficulty in getting to sleep. Finally, after praying, I drifted off, and I had a dream. I am satisfied that God has spoken to me only four times in my life through

dreams, but a dream like this one was no coincidence. It was from the Lord. When I woke up, I knew immediately what it meant.

In this dream it seemed that another minister and I were walking on some kind of parade ground or ball field. There were stands on either side of us. As we were walking along talking, the man jumped and exclaimed, "Look!"

I turned and saw two ferocious roaring lions. The man started running. I started running with him. Then I stopped and told him we were too far away from the stands to reach safety. We'd never escape those lions.

I stopped dead still, turned around, and went back to meet the lions. They came toward me with their fangs bared, roaring.

I was trembling. I told them, "I resist you in the Name of Jesus. In Jesus's Name you can't hurt me." I just stood there. They ran right up to me like a couple of kittens, sniffed around my ankles, and finally frolicked off, paying no attention to me.

Then I woke up. I knew exactly what God was saying to me. The Scripture in First Peter 5 came to me. It says, 'Be sober, be vigilant; because your adversary the devil, as a roaring lion, walketh about, seeking whom he may devour. Whom resist stedfast in the faith…' (Vv.8.9, KJV).

> The physical battle I had been fighting was won right then. Instantly the symptoms disappeared and I was all right. I had stood my ground. I wouldn't give in. I had won.[56]

## Catherine Marshall's Dream

In the preface to *A Man Called Peter*, Catherine Marshall tells of a dream she had after her husband, Peter's, death: "Peter was working in a rose garden and said playfully, 'I know perfectly well what you've been doing, Catherine. You're writing a book.... It's all right, Kate. Go ahead and write it. Tell it all, if it will prove to people that a man can love the Lord and not be a sissy...'"[57] Filled with wonderful humor, wisdom, and loving detail, the powerful story of Peter Marshall's life has touched the hearts and minds of millions of people. It is a book about love—the love between a dynamic man and his God, and the tender, romantic love between a man and the woman he married. It is also the gripping adventure of a poor Scottish immigrant who became chaplain of the United States Senate and one of the most revered men in America.

## A visitor's Dream with a Message for St. Augustine

Shortly before Augustine's death, Roman Africa was overrun by the Vandals, a warlike tribe with Arian sympathies. They had entered Africa at the instigation of Count Boniface, but soon turned to lawlessness, plundering private citizens and churches and killing many of the inhabitants. The Vandals arrived in the spring of 430 to besiege Hippo and during that time, Augustine endured his final illness.

Possidius records that one of the few miracles attributed to Augustine took place during the siege. While Augustine was confined to his sick bed, a man petitioned him to lay his hands upon a relative who was ill. Augustine replied that if he had any power to cure the sick, he would surely have applied it to himself first. The visitor declared that he was told in a dream to go to Augustine so that his relative would be made whole. When Augustine heard this, he no longer hesitated, but laid his hands upon the sick man, who departed from Augustine's presence, healed.[58]

## Pope John Paul II's Dream of the Homeless Cats

In 1984, author Anton Gronowicz wrote a book entitled *God's Broker,* which was the result of two hundred hours' worth of conversation with Pope John Paul II. The book's subtitle is *The Life of John Paul II as Told in His Own Words* and contains a dream the Pope had on a night in 1969 before his first visit to New York City. The author of *God's Broker* wrote, at the conclusion of the Pope's telling of his dream, "I had never seen such a sad expression on the face of this man." He could tell that the dream had a deep impact on the Pope. Later the Pope made a pilgrimage to Assisi, the birthplace of St. Francis, where he spoke about people's *solicitous care* toward animals and nature in general. Because of the homeless cat dream, the Pontiff could relate somewhat to St. Francis and his love for animals, as well as human beings. And he likened that love to the coming kingdom where all, both humans and animals, will live in eternal peace with each other (Isaiah 11:6, 65:25).

The following is the Pontiff's dream in his own words:

> It was a terribly severe winter in New York; the city was completely covered with snow. Inhabitants were well off and warmly dressed and walking slowly along roads because cars, due to mountains of snow, could not be operated. I was happy that I could walk on top of the snow on avenues of white.
>
> All my physical effort was spent on walking. To this day, pictures of huge apartment houses on both sides of the avenue are instilled in my mind and the doormen quickly closing and opening entrance doors as though trying to prevent humanity and warmth from escaping.
>
> On top of the snow, I noticed a brown cat emerge from a side street and walk on the snow. I looked closer and, to my surprise, saw that this big cat was being followed by six small brown-and-white kittens, all of them following the big brown cat in a perfect line. The mother cat looked back from time to time to see if her babies were there, but her main concern was to reach the entrance door. I presumed she was trying to find warmth for herself and her children, but as soon as she reached the door, a man

in a well-pressed uniform jumped at her with a broom and chased them away. I followed this procession and prepared to deliver a speech to the doorman. I opened my mouth and tried to complain, "Where is your proverbial American generosity? Where is your American good heart and fair play? Let them in. Let them in!"

I tried to speak, but the words would not come out. Maybe I was afraid of the doorman with the broom. I started searching my cassock pockets for a piece of bread, found some crumbs, and put them on my palms, calling, "Kitty, kitty, kitty." But the words would not come from my supposedly intelligent mouth. Instead, the wind blew the crumbs from my palm, and I said, "What can I do? I can't speak to the cats. I can't speak to the doorman. But there are many hungry birds. They might pick up the crumbs."

Again, I walked after the cats, now with a pain in my chest, feeling tremendous cold. On the left, I saw a church building and thought, "There we will find help." I heard singing, and again, the idea occurred to me that it must be a Catholic church. The music grew louder, as though trying to convince God that they were praying to Him.

The mother cat jumped in front of me and climbed the stairs, followed by her kittens. I raised my head and saw a tall Jesuit priest chasing the cats off the steps. But as I was about to shout at the Jesuit, "I am a cardinal!" and give an order to accept the cats, the mother cat and her offspring ran behind the church because from there came the appetizing aroma of food. Probably there was a kitchen there. But a second Jesuit appeared at the kitchen door and scared the cats away. They returned to the avenue and started walking north.

They walked on the same side of the avenue as the Jesuit church and I followed. Then they reached an imposing red brick church. An Anglican bishop appeared and said to the cats, "My dear animal children, please go immediately to the animal shelter. There is food for you there. We Anglican clergy donate lots of money to the animal shelter every year at Christmastime."

The mother cat and her kittens didn't even meow. They knew the authoritative voice of the Anglican bishop. They walked uptown and gradually the luxurious buildings disappeared, together with the doormen, and we saw drab dilapidated apartments.

As they walked and the buildings grew shabbier and dirty, a door was opened, not by a doorman but by an old wrinkled woman in a cotton dress. [She saw the cats] and shouted, 'Oh, little mother,' and when she opened her mouth, I saw she had few teeth. She gently ushered the mother cat and kittens inside, who jumped happily about because the warmth of the house embraced them.[59]

By relating his dream in the book, *God's Broker,* Pope John Paul II has given witness to a need for the "solicitous care, not only of people, but of animals." God had given the Pontiff a dream with a message of love and compassion for His creatures.

In relating these stories of dreams given to famous people I hope to stir up in you hope and excitement. For every famous person who had an important dream there are millions of people just like you and me who dream every night and also hear God in our dreams. God is not a respecter of persons. He loves all of His children. Whether you are famous or not so famous, God is speaking to you in your dreams. All you need to do is tune your heart and your ears toward Him.

# Chapter 9: How the Dream Was Lost to the Church and How It Can Be Recovered

> ...I could uncover little on the subject [dream interpretation] in Christian literature. The Church for the most part was ignoring the subject. This was strange when we consider the thread of dream material all through the Bible.[60]
>
> Catherine Marshall
> *Something More*

In 1980, my spiritual director asked me what God was telling me in my dreams. At that time I did not know. And I was embarrassed not to know. No one in my life had ever asked me that question. I had been in church since the cradle and not one person at church had asked me anything about my dreams. Each morning I remembered my dreams, but I did not know I was supposed to write them down. No one I knew at that time wrote their dreams down, and no one talked about the fact that they dreamed anything. I was a dream journal virgin.

After this encounter with my spiritual director, she talked with me about dreams, and my eyes were opened to a new world. It was as if I had always seen the world in black and white, and now I saw in vivid Technicolor.

I asked her to give me names of some books I could read on the subject, and she gave me the name of one book. From there I searched for every Christian book I could find on dreams. I found five.

God had blessed me with this particular spiritual director because she was very knowledgeable about dreams. After a few years she was holding dream workshops in the Dallas/Fort Worth area, and I attended every one of them. I faithfully kept my dream journal, and soon I was being asked to speak to small groups of women about dreams. I devoured books by Morton Kelsey and John Sanford and was hungry for more. The New Age books on the shelf held no interest for me. My true hunger was for God and the Holy Spirit and how I could get closer to both of them. I knew that New Age books were not the truth, and I wouldn't waste time with them. I wanted to be fed God's Word and His truth on the matter of dreams. One of the first things I did was to read through the New Testament and highlight every dream in green ink. After that I tackled the Old Testament, which took awhile. But eventually I knew for myself what the Bible had to say about dreams. It was quite a bit more than I ever imagined, and I had read the Bible since childhood.

So if the Bible had a lot to say about dreams, why didn't the Church say anything about them? When my priest heard I was learning about dreams, he asked me to speak to a group of women. He confessed to me that he didn't know anything about dreams, and he wanted to sit in on the group. It was the first time I had ever spoken in front of a group. However, the group was intrigued with the subject matter, and soon they were asking questions and holding a vigorous discussion. From that first group I was asked to speak to groups in Sunday Schools, Anglican groups of Daughters of the King, healing missions, and other gatherings. People were like me. They had no idea that God spoke to people through their dreams or that they could hear His quiet voice in the night while they slept.

Soon I found that the Church had abandoned teaching about dreams or even believing in the ability to hear God through them. Pastors did not know about dreams or many other aspects of the soul. In the modern church, matters of the soul had been relegated to psychologists, psychiatrists, or social workers. What was once the specialty of the pastor as healer of the soul had become sicknesses that only a *professional* was equipped to handle.

As the realization of this began to bother me, I asked myself, "Are people healthier in their souls now that they see professionals? Or would they be better with Godly spiritual directors who can lead them to the feet of Jesus where they can be touched by the One who created them?" How many Christians see counselors who are not Christians? Even though Psalm 1:1 says, "How blessed is the man who does not walk in the counsel of the wicked…" Some may say, "Yes, but my pastor is not a trained psychologist." That may be, but he was trained in God's Word and filled with the Holy Spirit. Wherever the Holy Spirit's activity is demonstrated, people are healed and changed.

## Early Church Fathers Still Listening to God in Their Dreams

Throughout the Bible there are accounts of dreams. Some dream experts believe that part of the Apostle John's Revelation that he wrote in AD 95 or 96 may have been a dream. But evidence shows that from creation until now, God has not stopped speaking to His people through their dreams.

One of John's disciples, Polycarp, pastor of the church in Smyrna, had a prophetic dream on the night before he was martyred. In the dream his pillow was on fire, and he knew what the dream meant. On waking he told his fellow believers, "I must be burned alive." The next day on February 23 in AD 155 he was brought into the public games where the crowd had brought firewood and kindling from their woodshops to build the fire. While standing on the firewood Polycarp said, "You threaten me with the fire that burns for a time and is quickly quenched, but you do not know the fire that awaits the wicked and the judgment to come into everlasting punishment. Come and do what you will."[61] Amazingly, the fire never burned Polycarp as he stood on the wood pile and sang praises to God. Finally, his captors grew weary of him and thrust through him with spears.

There are many other early church fathers who understood their dreams and related them to others. St. Ambrose, the Bishop of Milan, born in AD 370, was admonished in a dream to search for and find, under the pavement of the church, the remains of two martyrs.[62]

In the history books of Nicene Fathers there is no one more honored than Gregory of Nyssa, born in AD 335 and younger brother of Basil the Great. But while a young man he also was admonished by a dream. His mother had asked him to attend a service of honor for the holy Forty Martyrs, so he traveled a long way to comply. However, he was so tired from the journey that he fell asleep during the ceremony. During his nap he had a dream where the Forty Martyrs appeared to him and threatened him and reproached him for his slothfulness. When he awoke, he quickly repented and worked diligently for the Lord thereafter.[63]

The third-century priest Tertullian not only believed in the power of the dream he wrote about it. In his book entitled *A Treatise on the Soul*, he devoted eight chapters to sleep and dreams. He discounted the notion that dreams had any connection at all to what the dreamer had to eat or whether he had eaten at all like some people believed at that time. He wrote that the body and soul were independent of each other and that the soul is immortal.[64]

Like Tertullian, Synesius of Cyrene also wrote about dreams, but later in the fifth century. His book, *On Dreams*, was one of the best of its kind at that time. He believed even then that dreams are personal and each person should interpret their dreams according to their own inner symbols rather than relying on dream symbol dictionaries. Synesius kept a dream journal and encouraged the practice in others.[65]

Before Jerome was ordained he still read pagan classics until he had a dream that turned his life around.

During an illness, he dreamed he stood before the tribunal of Christ.

"Thou a Christian?" asked the judge skeptically. "Thou art a Ciceronian. Where thy treasure is, there thy heart is also."

He repented of this habit, and it was not long after that when he was ordained. Jerome was a priest, scholar, secretary to a pope, author, translator, monk, and recluse. The Church regards him as the greatest of all the doctors in clarifying the Divine Word.[66]

## The Dark Ages of Dreams

From the early church fathers until AD 1200, dreams were an integral part of the church's teaching and life in the spirit. The dream was still essential in knowledge of diagnosing illness. Dreams were listened to for prophesy, for warnings, and for God's correction in the church. Those who listened to their dreams held a special level of spirituality that was lacking in those who knew nothing about tapping into the mind of God in that way. Almost every popular saint, early church father, and religious writer wrote about at least one dream that affected their lives. From warning dreams to revelation dreams, the saints listened to their dreams, remembered them, wrote them down, and passed them on. So how could such an essential avenue to God have its very life's blood closed off to the modern church?

My research revealed there were three important people whose scholarly efforts set the whole sad state of affairs in motion. First there was the great philosopher Aristotle. His contributions were many in the areas of science, chemistry, biology, zoology and botany. The theory of logic was original with him. Also, the idea of the *unmovable mover* was his theory of God. But he was a man of science. Sadly, he had no use for mysticism or spirituality.[67] He rejected the idea that dreams had a divine origin. His theories about dreams were outlined in three books: *On Dreams*; *On Sleep and Waking*; and *On Prophecy in Sleep*. In spite of Aristotle's interest in dreams, he claimed that the only way for humans to know reality was by sense experience. He denounced the idea that dreams could provide any information about the divine.

In AD 382 dreams took another blow when Jerome translated the entire Bible into Latin and deliberately translated the Hebrew word for witchcraft, *anan*, as *observing dreams*. He did not mistranslate the word every time, however. He only did it three times out of ten. If there is any doubt that Jerome did this on purpose, we can only suppose that since he knew what the correct translation was for seven times, then he more than likely knew what it was the other three times. As a result, Jerome's mistranslations changed the course of Christian belief and practice regarding dreams.

When Thomas Aquinas was writing his authoritative text for the Catholic Church, *Summa Theologica*, in the thirteenth century he attempted to clear up some of the mistakes of Jerome and concluded that there were four causes of dreams: two inward ones, arising from daytime preoccupations and from physical humors, and two outward ones, arising either from God or demons.[68] However, Aquinas was torn between the Church and the Philosopher. When it came to taking a stand for the Bible and its teaching about dreams, Aquinas fell short. He finally came down on the side of translating Christianity and the Bible "into the language of Aristotle."[69] Unfortunately, the *Summa Theologica* became the authoritative text of the Catholic Church from the thirteenth century until the second Vatican Council in the mid-1960s.

## From Aquinas and Freud

Dreams were dealt a severe blow by Aquinas when he issued warnings that dreams could either be given by God or by demons. As a result the church became obsessed with demons and devils. Even Martin Luther seemed to fear the presence of demons around every corner, as can be seen in the movie *Luther*. From the 1500s to the 1800s, people were encouraged by the church to actively suppress their dreams and remembering them. In fact, remembering one's dreams and talking about them became a matter of life and death. Dreamers could be severely tortured, and some were burned at the stake.

## Freud, Jung, and Exit of Dreams from the Church

In Dr. Robert Van de Castle's book *Our Dreaming Mind*, Dr. Van de Castle writes extensively about the dream theorists of the nineteenth century. He states that the "enlightenment philosophy," along with the industrial revolution, "put an increasing emphasis on material goods and productivity."[70] As a result the Romantic School developed in opposition, which stressed mysticism and, as a by-product, dreams. Several essayists, physicians, and scientists wrote books about dreams and the unconscious.

But none was as important as the book *The Interpretation of Dreams*, written by Sigmund Freud in 1900. Freud was both a scientist and a physician. He was also a rationalist, and he insisted that dreams were also rational. As important as Freud's dream book was, it did nothing to help the church draw nearer to God. Freud was not a Christian and in fact called himself a "hopeless pagan."[71]

C. G. Jung, on the other hand, believed that dreams were symbolic and that the language they spoke was also symbolic. Jung wrote extensively for fifty years about his findings concerning the unconscious and how we can learn to understand how it speaks to us. In 1983, while attending a dream workshop in Dallas, Texas, I saw a black-and-white film of an interview with C. G. Jung, and he appeared to be in his eighties. The interviewer asked him if he believed in God. His answer was interesting. He answered, "I don't believe in God. I know God."

Sigmund Freud, I believe, helped greatly in the abandonment of spiritual counseling by pastors in the church. From my research I learned that Freud knew that if mental problems could be taken out of the hands of pastors, then religion would have little to do with dreams and the unconscious. From Freud forward, any problems of the soul were no longer associated with sin but are all diagnosed as illnesses. If church members are then thought of as sick rather than sinners, then their care and treatment must be handed over to healthcare givers. As a result, fewer and fewer pastors are doing spiritual counseling. Fewer pastors are preaching about sin, forgiveness, and absolution. Rather church members are being sent to psychiatrists and mental health counselors where they may stay in treatment for years. Sometimes a better approach would be confronting the church member with the Word of God and letting the Holy Spirit do the healing of the person's mind and soul.

When spiritual counseling is taken out of the hands of the pastor or spiritual director, then also is the work of listening to God through our dreams. In fact, listening to God at all may be trivialized or discouraged by a secular mental health professional. Freud himself predicted what would happen with his plan. In a letter to Pfister he wrote, "The cure of souls…will one day be a recognized non-ecclesiastical and even nonreligious calling."[72] He was obviously right. The cure of souls has now become the job of the healthcare system and not the church. Unfortunately, the cure of souls also includes listening to dreams.

## Two Important Witnesses in the Church—Kelsey and Sanford

After Sigmund Freud and C. G. Jung, there were two Episcopal priests who brought light about dreams back into Christianity and the church. Morton T. Kelsey and

John A. Sanford are the authors of several books about dreams and the seemingly pioneers of dream work in the twentieth century. Morton T. Kelsey was a professor at Notre Dame, and he wrote *Dark Speech of the Spirit* (which is now titled *God, Dreams, and Revelation*) in 1968. After that he wrote *Dreams: A Way to Listen to God* and other books. He also gave lectures and advice to a myriad of people about the study of dreams. One of his main purposes was to offer practical suggestions for modern Christians about understanding their dreams and about knowing the "reality of the spiritual world and Jesus Christ who is the victor there."

For more than twenty years Morton T. Kelsey and John A. Sanford were friends and fellow trailblazers on the path to understanding dreams in the modern church. Sanford's first book about dreams, *Dreams: God's Forgotten Language* was published in 1968. After that, later books were published including *Dreams and Healing* and *The Invisible Partners*. Gradually after Kelsey and Sanford western Christian theologians began to take an interest in dreams, and more dream books were published. But it was still not easy.

Both Kelsey and Sanford talk about the difficulty they encountered in getting their respective books published. In fact, both of them published their first books on the subject in a roundabout way through publishers in Germany, not in America. John Sanford wrote his first dream book while serving as an Army Reserve chaplain. After he wrote the book his path led him to the Jung Institute in Zurich for further study. At that time the Institute offered to publish his book in

German, which meant that it first had to be translated from English to German.

Later after many rejections an American publisher did publish the book and after a television interview Sanford finally received national interest in his first book about dreams.

Interestingly, Morton T. Kelsey's second book also started from roots in Germany, not in America. He was lecturing in western Germany in 1973, in English, but the translator took the tapes of the lecture and translated them into a small book in German. That book was published in Germany in 1974. Later, after many requests for materials on his lecture and interest in the book, he obtained the original tapes of the lectures and a friend translated the German book back into English with the help of the tapes.

It is amazing and wonderful that these two modern day Christian dream scholars had their work about dreams published in the 1960s and 70s. Those books have led the way in the western church for interest in the spiritual lives of humans, in contact with God through our dreams, and in further interest in the unconscious and how it aids us toward healing.

## The Church's Call to Heal the Soul

Every time I speak to a group about dreams, they seem genuinely hungry to know about the subject matter. If the subject comes up at dinner, everyone stops eating and listens. It seems that everyone is interested in dreams. People are curious about dreams, where they come from, and what they mean. They want to hear about your dreams, and they want to tell at least one of theirs. What is this tug in our hearts toward dreams? I believe that it may not be about dreams themselves but about a hunger we have for real contact with God. Something inside all of us wants to have a real experience with God. And we all suspect that God has something to do with dreams.

"If I only touch his garment, I shall get well," said the woman with the issue of blood (Matthew 9:21). Don't we all believe that if we get close enough to Jesus we'll get well? It is difficult for people to realize that God does *not* talk to us through our dreams. They are so *other worldly*; surely they have something to do with God. The frustrating thing is we don't understand what He's trying to tell us! If that is true, and I believe it is, then why would we believe that a psychiatrist rather than a pastor would be able to lead us to the One Who is the Healer of all?

If God created us, and He wants to talk to us, who would be the *professional* spiritual person to lead us to Him? The one who is called by God and anointed to help us hear from God. Those persons would be pastors, priests, monks, nuns, and spiritual directors. If a layman in the church begins having dreams that point him or her toward a certain ministry, whom do they talk with about it? If you have a vision or an unusual spiritual experience, who do you call? There are very few spiritual directors today, but they can be found. Unfortunately, not very many people have access to monks or nuns. But you may be blessed to have a pastor or a priest who understands the things of the soul.

When I began to hear from God that He wanted me to be in the healing ministry, I knew nothing about what that meant. I did not know where to begin. It frightened me a little, thinking that I might be sent to a hospital to pray for people, and I didn't know how to begin. I didn't know if the hospital would allow me to have access to patients, or if the patients were open to someone walking into their room and asking if they wanted prayers. So I made an appointment with my priest. I asked him if he knew anything about the gift of healing or about the healing ministry of the church. I told him about my unusual experiences of laying my hands on people and praying. He was very quiet.

Then he said, "I don't know anything about this sort of thing, but I will find out. When I know something to tell you, I'll call, and we can get back together."

I was blessed to have a priest who was open-minded enough to find out what he didn't have personal knowledge of. As it turned out he read books, and he talked with his bishop, and he called me for another appointment.

He told me what he had learned, and he asked me if I was willing to make hospital visits with him and learn how to be a volunteer chaplain from our church. I began to go with him, and he taught me how to make hospital visits, how to pray for people who were seriously ill, and how to become an asset to the hospital visiting ministry. Soon I was visiting two hospitals every week laying hands on and praying for people as God led me to do.

I was fortunate to have a priest and a bishop who understood spiritual experiences. What they didn't know, they found out for me. We all learned new things of God together. When God began to speak to me clearly through my dreams, I attended area dream workshops to learn more. As I learned, my priest asked me to speak to small women's groups about what I learned. And he sat in on the meetings in order to learn, too. What a blessing to have a spiritual authority, a shepherd over me, who was humble enough to admit he didn't know everything, and who was willing to submit himself to the new knowledge of his lambs.

## How the Church Can Draw Nearer to God with its Dreams

The sad truth about the church today is that many pastors and priests are not called by God to be in the position they are in. They only have a job. They may even have what they call a career. Maybe they had an emotional experience when they were young, and they made a decision to become a pastor. Or maybe they were *mother-called*, *father-called*, or *grandmother-called*. However it happened, many are not God-called. If you ask them to tell you about their calling, they mumble and stumble around and never tell you how God actually called them, because He didn't.

And because they weren't called by God, their ministry is not anointed. There is no power in their sermons. No power in their prayers. As a result some churches are barely hanging on. Only by sheer will power are the doors being kept open and the bills paid. No one is getting healed. No lives are changed by the Holy Spirit.

In churches such as this, sermons are lifeless and the members are sick and not prosperous. They long for something more but don't know what it is. The problem is their foundation is wrong. If there is no anointing on the pastor, he cannot impart a real experience with the Lord. Yes, he can preach a sermon. He can be a nice guy and can hold together a church that acts like a country club. But in order for there to be power from on high the pastor needs to be one that is God called and God anointed. He should be filled with the Holy Spirit with signs, wonders, and miracles following (Hebrews 2:4). When a church is blessed to have this kind of pastor, he will preach with power from God's Holy Word, and he'll have revelation knowledge. As a result revelation knowledge will also come through dreams. As in the Bible, men who were close to God were the recipients of God's wisdom in all kinds of ways, including dreams. God spoke to those men when they were awake and when they were asleep. And it still happens today.

The church and its shepherds should not be afraid of dreams. Nor should it be afraid to know what is in the soul of man. After all the church is in the business of reconciliation, which involves sin, confession, and forgiveness. Confession involves telling another person about what is in our mind and our heart. We should be able to unburden our soul to our pastor. In return he should tell us what Jesus would tell us if He were here in the flesh. Ridding ourselves of evil thoughts and evil deeds helps us lay down our burdens at the feet of Jesus. As sin passes away, righteousness is invited in. Our confessor knows how or should know how to lead us toward this goal. This is not the role of a psychiatrist or a psychologist. It is the role of a man or woman of God.

When we refuse to face the sin in our lives, it mounts up. Things begin to go wrong. We lose our jobs. Our kids end up in trouble. We may turn to drugs or alcohol. The church loses its attractiveness as a safe haven. We withhold ourselves from God and other Christians. Reading the Bible seems like a chore instead of a treasure hunt. We get bored with Christianity. So where do we turn?

If we are Christians, then we should know at least one friend who we feel is a brother or sister in Christ. A phone call is difficult sometimes, but someone may know someone else who has a spiritual director. Some churches call them spiritual coaches. A spiritual director is able to listen without judging and tell you what the Bible says about your situation.

Do you need a word from God? Do you need a touch from Jesus? An anointed spiritual director can put you in touch with divine knowledge and power. Time and time again I get phone calls from people who say, "I believe God told me to call you. I'm not sure why except that I need some answers." And I truly believe that my job as a spiritual director is to help the directed hear God's voice. It may take repentance and a changing of some behavior patterns. It may take creating some holy rituals that will turn your heart and mind toward God's perpetual presence.

But it will definitely take listening to God through your dreams. Even if you've never remembered a dream in your life, it is possible to begin slowly and create a snowball of journal entries with revelation knowledge straight from God. And don't we all want a real experience with God? Don't we want more than a weak walk with the Lord? Yes, I'm convinced that most Christians want more than they're experiencing at the moment. We long for the abundant life that Jesus talked about in John 10:10.

Knowledge is wonderful. We all want more knowledge. If we didn't, Wikipedia would be out of business. If we didn't want to know more and more, we'd stop buying iPads and laptops that can take us on a mental ride on the Internet highway. But God says this, "Call to Me, and I will answer you, and I will tell you great and mighty things, which you do not know" (Jeremiah 33:3). How many of us do this? Do we ask God when we're stumped on how to do something or do we whiz right over to ehow.com for the answers? God gave us minds to use. That's true. But when we need real answers to life's questions, how do we get those answers from God?

I submit that keeping a journal is an excellent way to see with our hearts and our spirits. In fact, I believe it is very difficult to figure out what God is telling us on a day-to-day basis without keeping a journal. If we try continually to figure out in our heads what God is telling us, we may never know. But if we can get it down on paper in front of our eyes, all of a sudden everything becomes clear. The old phrase, "A picture is worth a thousand words" becomes very true. As a spiritual director I ask my directees to add to their journals poems they write, dreams they have, doodles they draw, songs they get on their minds and can't get rid of, and names of people that keep crossing their paths over and over. The reason is: God will use anything in this world to get through to you. He will speak to you through billboards, bumper stickers, radio DJs, and anything else that you pay attention to in order to tell you something. So the more you put into your journal, the better chance you have of getting the message.

The great thing about a journal is that you can go back and see long patterns. Those patterns may have begun three months ago, and they were so subtle they went right over your head. But after some time passes, you can flip back through old entries, and *Voila!* There it is. You never saw it before, but over and over and over again there it is—the same word, the same picture, the same sound. And the realization hits you that God is trying to tell you something!

When the church wakes up to the fact that God wants to tell it things just as badly as it wants to hear from Him, then it will finally figure out ways to make a real connection with Him! I believe that it is not only one solution. God is much more complex than that. If you don't hear Him one way, He'll come at you from some other way. You might start having a repeating dream. You'll have it over and over and just when you think it's gone, you'll have it again. If you don't write it down, you might miss subtle changes in the dream from one time to another. You might think they're all alike when they're not. There is more depth to you than you realize. One dream might reveal one truth on one level and another deeper truth on a deeper level. But you won't realize this unless you write it down.

Who is the church? The body of Christ, and Paul says that one person is a foot, one is a hand, one is an eye, etc. (1 Corinthians 12:12-20). Maybe not everyone will listen to their dreams and understand them, but someone will. If you don't, find someone who does who can help you. Ask God to send someone to you who has an ear to hear Him. Ask in faith, and you will receive (Matthew 21:22). The church must wake up and hear the voice of God. I pray continually that the church will not be satisfied to be *asleep in the light.* Yes, we have revelation knowledge as His children. But do we know it? Do we experience it? Or are we walking around in a fog just wondering why God doesn't talk to us.

If our early church fathers listened to their dreams and tried to figure out what God was saying, then why don't we do the same? God says in Jeremiah 29:11 (NIV), "I know the plans I have for you, plans to prosper you and not harm you, plans to give you hope and a future." Do you know what those plans are? Do you want to know? Or are you waiting for someone else to tell you what they are? Are you waiting for Joel Osteen or Joyce Meyers to tell you what God's plans are for you? I hope not. Yes, those ministers are wonderful instruments of God. Yes, they have knowledge and power. But God can talk to you just like He talks to them. You can hear God at your personal level. So can your pastor. So can your whole church.

Some churches or members of churches have a prejudice against learning about things of the soul. People get lazy. They aren't interested in learning something knew. They had rather hold onto what they've learned in the past. Maybe they are afraid of God or what He might tell them. They don't want to actually get that close to Him. He might require that they change. And changing is hard. The question is: do you want a dead religion or one that is alive and powerful? How far are you willing to go to have that kind of relationship with God?

When God says, "I know the plans I have for you…" does that frighten you? Are you thinking, "Oh my gosh, He could send me to Africa as a missionary. Then what would I do?" For one thing, that's probably not going to happen. For another thing, God loves you so much if He did send you to Africa to be a missionary then He would equip you, and He would bless you beyond anything you can think of if you chose to obey and go. Why is it we always think that God will give us something to do that we'll hate? Why couldn't it be something that we'll love doing? God's plans for us could include learning a new trade or living in a better city or making more money or meeting new people, better people. If God loves us, why would He want to make us unhappy? He wouldn't.

The question is still the same as it was in the Garden of Eden. Will we obey God or will we do what we want to do. Will God be Lord of our lives, or will we? Will we choose to walk with Him in the cool of day and have fellowship with the Creator of the universe or will we be satisfied to wander around aimlessly not knowing where we are going?

After Adam and Eve sinned in the Garden, God came to do just that, like He did from time to time, walk and talk with them in the cool of the day (Genesis 3:8). But they hid themselves from His presence, and He had to ask, "Where are you?" Did God know where they were? Surely He did. But did they? Did they know where they were in relationship to God at that moment? I don't think they did. "Where are you?" God asked. He could ask us all today. He could ask the whole church today. "Where are you church? Do you know?"

Are you listening to God and obeying His voice? Are you healing the sick in their bodies and souls? Are you magnifying and testifying God's Holy Word in your life? Or are you hiding yourself from walking and talking with Him?

The church must find pastors, priests, nuns, monks, and spiritual directors who have been called (and there are many), and filled with His Holy Spirit and anointed to lead the church down the path that leads to the tree of life, the life that is abundant and full and powerful. Not only should the church be hearing His voice, the church should also be following His voice and telling everyone they know what He's saying. When that happens, it'll be interesting to see if He is telling the church the same things all over the world. When God has a message, He reveals it to more than one person, more than one congregation, more than one body. If the church would start comparing notes instead of keeping the truth to itself, walls would come down, the Spirit would flow freely, and Christians would live in harmony, health, and prosperity. The kingdom would actually come on the earth as it is in heaven.

# Chapter 10: Drawing Nearer to God–Time to Take Action

> High achievers spot rich opportunities swiftly, make big decisions quickly and move into action immediately. Follow these principles and you can make your dreams come true.
>
> Robert H. Schuller
> Evangelist, Hour of Power

Now that you know how important dreams are to God and to you, what will you do? You could make up your mind to get started today by buying a journal or a notebook, inserting paper, and start writing down your dreams, but why would you want to do that? Isn't that work? You could tell your friends about what you learned but they might think you're strange. You could talk to your pastor or priest about this book and recommend that they read it, too, but they might not listen to you. You could finish reading this book, make up your mind to try all of the suggestions in order to find out what God wants to do with your life, but that might be scary. Besides you're a busy person. You have a job and a family and sports and hobbies and a million things going on in your life.

I hope you won't let a lot of *buts* in your vocabulary stop you from having the life God wants you to have. That would be sad. Whether you bought this book or checked it out of the library or borrowed it from a friend, it must have drawn you in some way. Something about the title or the cover must have spoken to you deep in your soul. Or maybe you were just curious. If you've gotten this far in reading it and haven't tossed it aside yet, then maybe Someone is trying to tell you something.

When I begin doing spiritual direction with a directee, I tell them, "Eighty percent of people don't get what they want because they don't know what they want."

Besides wanting a house, a car, a family, a great job—the basics—most people don't know exactly what it is that will make them happy. They just know that what they have now is not it. They're looking for whatever that something is. Maybe they think it's money. If they just had enough money, extra money, they could buy a getaway house, and then they'd have time to relax and figure it all out. They could sit by the lake and drink a cool glass of something fruity and God would talk to them, and it'd become instantly clear what it is that is missing from their lives. That intangible hole that they've tried to fill with everything from sports, to diets, to spa trips, to extreme adventures, is never filled. Nothing so far has worked. More than likely nothing will fill that hole in anyone's soul until they draw close to God and He fills it. Having God fill your soul is like having streams of living water flowing freely and consistently, always refreshing because they are not stagnant (John 4:10, 13-14).

That's the good news. In fact, that's the fantastic news! Now here's the hard news: whenever we decide to step out in faith and take a chance with God, something rises up in us that tries to keep us back. There is a resistance that comes, and with resistance comes excuses why we shouldn't do what God is calling us to do. Sometimes that resistance is our comfort zone, sometimes it's fear—fear of failing, fear of succeeding. Resistance might be as simple as not being able to find the right journal you want. Maybe you keep forgetting your dreams. Maybe you don't have a night-light, or your spouse doesn't support your new efforts. Your inner list could go on and on. Whatever the resistance is you run up against, make up your mind in the very beginning to move ahead anyway. Armed with determined resolve, you set your face toward the goal, and an almost invisible shield moves out ahead of you. It will shove obstacles out of your way very soon, and they will fall at your side. When your face is set toward a goal, life steps up to help you at every turn. Forces in the universe come to your aid that you never imagined before. It is almost like your brain is magnetized toward what you want, once you know what that is, and forces in nature begin to draw it to you. When you know and make up your mind to draw nearer to God, God and everything in His kingdom start drawing nearer to you (James 4:8).

## If You Are Afraid of God

Some people take the scripture in Hebrews the wrong way. When the writer of Hebrews 10:31 (NJKV), wrote,

"It is a fearful thing to fall into the hands of the living God," perhaps he wasn't saying that being close to God is terrifying. But maybe you're thinking, "Sure, he was. God is, after all, able to kill people." It is true God has wiped out entire cities. The city of Sodom realized His power when He sent down fire and brimstone from heaven (Genesis 19:24). When Moses was leading Israel out of Egypt toward the promised land, God caused Miriam to become leprous when she spoke against His servant, Moses, and his authority (Number 12:10). Even Jesus warned in Matthew 10:28 (KJV), "And fear not them which kill the body, but are not able to kill the soul: but rather fear Him which is able to destroy both soul and body in hell." Why would anyone want to get close to a God who is terrifying?

The answer is: because of His love. If you are in Christ Jesus, then God is not angry with you. God does nothing that is not about His love for us. Even if we can't see it at first, when we look closer we realize that with God, it *is* all about us. You may have heard the current saying, "God loves you so much that your picture is on His refrigerator door." That is true. Your picture is also in His wallet. He brags to all of His friends about you. When you were conceived, it was love at first sight.

Because we are loved, we are drawn to the One who loves us. After all, there is no one else who loves us as much as God. No one else gave His son to die for us while we were yet sinners (Romans 5:8). God Himself tells us how much He loves us over and over again in the scriptures. But nothing says it as passionately as Ezekiel 16:1-14, when God was speaking about His love for Israel and its people when He was trying to bring them back from their disobedience into a loving relationship again with Him. His voice is full of devotion and adoration for a people He wants to have mercy on. This is the God we serve.

> Thus says the Lord God to Jerusalem, "Your origin and your birth are from the land of the Canaanite, your father was an Amorite and your mother a Hittite. As for your birth, on the day you were born your navel cord was not cut, nor were you washed with water for cleansing; you were not rubbed with salt or even wrapped in cloths. No eye looked with pity on you to do any of these things for you, to have compassion on you. Rather you were thrown out into the open field, for you were abhorred on the day you were born. When I passed by you and saw you squirming in your blood, I said to you while you were in your blood, 'Live!' I said to you while you were in your blood, 'Live!'
>
> "I made you numerous like plants of the field. Then you grew up, became tall, and reached the age for fine ornaments; your breasts were formed and your hair had grown. Yet you were naked and bare. Then I passed by you and saw you, and behold, you were at the time for love; so I spread my skirt over you and covered your nakedness. I also swore to you and entered into a covenant with you so that you became Mine," declares the Lord God.

> "Then I bathed you with water, washed off your blood from you, and anointed you with oil. I also clothed you with embroidered cloth, and put sandals of porpoise skin on your feet; and I wrapped you with fine linen and covered you with silk. And I adorned you with ornaments, put bracelets on your hands, and a necklace around your neck.
>
> "'I also put a ring in your nostril, earrings in your ears, and a beautiful crown on your head. Thus you were adorned with gold and silver, and your dress was of fine linen, silk, and embroidered cloth. You ate fine flour, honey, and oil; so you were exceedingly beautiful and advanced to royalty. Then your fame went forth among the nations on account of your beauty, for it was perfect because of My splendor which I bestowed on you,' declares the Lord God.

These verses were spoken to Israel but the love He has for Israel is the same kind of love He bestows on us, those that love Him. "Behold, what manner of love the Father hath bestowed upon us, that we should be called the sons of God…" (1 John 3:1 KJV). Is there any doubt that God loves us? I pray not.

If He loves us, we should want to draw near to Him. We should want to spend time with Him and be in His presence. Have we really understood how much God wants to be with us? When He created the world, He came to Adam and Eve in the Garden and walked and talked with them in the cool of the day (Genesis 3:8). Later when the children of Israel were wandering in the wilderness God gave instructions for the building of the tabernacle, and He came to reside there (Exodus 25:8). Later still when the temple was built, God's glory filled the whole temple (2 Chronicles 5:14-6:1-2). Then He came to earth as a man and lived among us in the flesh (John 1:14). After Jesus was crucified, buried, and resurrected, God sent His Holy Spirit to reside within us (1 Corinthians 6:19). How can we doubt that He wants to be with us!

Therefore, how can we draw closer to Him? There are many ways. Foremost, we can talk to Him in prayer. We can listen to Him in meditation. We can spend time with Him in solitude and silence. We can hear him in our dreams.

## If You Feel Guilty

Guilt is the anger we feel toward ourselves for doing something we believe is wrong or for doing nothing when we knew we should have acted. It is the condemnation of our conscience because we violated our own rules of conduct. But guilt is not rational. It works whether our rules are rational or not. Do you feel guilty when you want to try something new? Why? Do you not feel that you deserve a chance to succeed at something?

Maybe someone else has tried to make you feel guilty, and you accepted the guilt. Maybe a friend or family member did not want you to pass them by with more blessings, with more prosperity, or with more of God in general. If you have let guilty feelings or guilty thoughts condemn you, let them go today! Refuse to let them hold you back from receiving all that God has to give you. Talk to God. Confess to Him that you have let family, friends, yourself, or the devil convince you that you are guilty when God Himself has set you free. Confess that you have let your guilty conscience hold you hostage to a life of lack when Jesus set you free from lack.

He said, "The Spirit of the Lord is upon Me, because He anointed Me to preach the gospel to the poor, He has sent me to proclaim release to the captives..." (Luke 4:18). That release came to you when you accepted Jesus as your Lord and Savior, because the captives were set free when He died on the cross. Tell God that you receive your release from guilt, and that you know now that you are innocent and not guilty. According to Romans 8:1, "There is therefore now no condemnation for those who are in Christ Jesus." So stop letting your conscience try to condemn you!

## If You Think You Are Unworthy

If you are in Christ Jesus, then unworthiness is a lie of the devil. The lie is that you are lacking in some way, that you are insufficient, not worth having what you want, not worth being successful, or not worth loving. It is a hideous lie and not biblical. In fact, the Bible says in Psalm 37:4, "Delight yourself in the Lord, and He will give you the desires of your heart." You *are* worthy to have what you want! God, counts you worthy to receive His blessings–the blessings of health, prosperity, success, and eternal life.

Jesus Christ makes us worthy not because of who we are but because Jesus made us worthy by dying for us. The truth is that we hold an inner treasure that surpasses greatness (2 Corinthians 4:7). We are worthy because Jesus bought us for a price (1 Corinthians 6:20). He paid with His life. Because of His death, burial, and resurrection we have become part of the body of Christ. The body of Christ is certainly worthy.

In John's Revelation we read about the heavenly throne, and the worship of the Lamb by the four living creatures and the twenty-four elders. They sing a song that says,

> Worthy art Thou to take the book, and to break its seals; for Thou wast slain, and didst purchase for God with Thy blood men from every tribe and tongue and people and nation. And Thou hast made them to be a kingdom and priests to our God; and they will reign upon the earth.
>
> Revelation 5:9

Those "men from every tribe and tongue and people and nation" are us, Christians! We are worthy because the one who purchased us is worthy! Please stop thinking today that you are unworthy. Take captive your thoughts and make them obedient to Christ Jesus (2 Corinthians 10:5). After all, you are the righteousness of God (2 Corinthians 5:21).

## Using Your Dreams to Get There

Because of who we are in Christ Jesus, we have a clear conscience, we are worthy, and we have no reason to be afraid of being close to God. Our very souls long to communicate with God, the One who is greater than ourselves. It is also more than communication, it is longing to absorb and savor God's presence. It is resting in a place that is otherworldly, the place of peace, the place of wonder and complete love. On some level we know in our hearts that there must be something more to this world than simply what we see. We may even sense that this world is not our home, that we belong somewhere else. And we long for that other place.

For years I have had a quote from *Mere Christianity* by the theologian C. S. Lewis on my desk. It reads, "If I find in myself a desire which no experience in this world can satisfy, the most probable explanation is that I was made for another world." Lewis was right. We *are* made for another world. That world is the world where God is. When we are dreaming, we touch that world for a few precious moments. During those moments we are living in a foreign country where we don't understand the language and where a lot of strangers surround us. That world is foreign to us only because we don't spend much time learning about it. We live in our outer, sense-perceptive world, rather than in our interior mystic world. Please do not make the mistake of thinking this is a fantasy world, because it is not. It is the real world of your soul. It is the one-third part of you other than your body and your spirit. You are not a body with a soul. Rather you are a soul with a body. Decide today that you will begin to listen to your soul through your dreams and begin to understand the dream language that God is speaking to you.

Keep a dream journal. Make a list of your own repeating dream symbols. Use your figuring-out skills to understand what your dreams are saying, and then decide to draw nearer to God using what He is telling you. It is a valuable tool at your disposal to understand your life, your purpose, and your destiny.

## Much Needed New Work of the Church

The Roman Catholic Church is better at interior work than the Protestants are. But the universal church must begin to believe in and value interior work. It needs to acknowledge that interior work is as valuable to a person's spiritual life as exterior work. Pastors, teachers, and leaders who create church programs need to enthusiastically create classes concerning prayer, meditation, journal keeping, and dreams. Anyone can learn these skills. If leaders in the church will promote learning these skills, others will join in. Church leaders should take the lead in communicating that the church values things of the soul. If the pastor or priest knows of someone in the church who is called by God to be a spiritual director, then that person should be asked to lead classes on interior work. All teachers should be called by God to teach. If they are, they will be anointed and so will be the things they teach. Discernment and confidentiality are absolute necessities for the teacher of these subjects.

## The Role of the Spiritual Director in the Church

One of the ways dreams can be brought back into the life of the church is if the role of the spiritual director is restored and if the spiritual director has knowledge sufficient to put people in touch with God through their dreams. The role of the spiritual director is to put people in touch with God so they can hear His voice. Of course, dreams should be a part of his/her knowledge. In its beginning spiritual direction was a concept borne for monastics. The spiritual director was a guide for those monks and nuns who left the monastery or convent to go live as hermits and solitaries. Since these Christians were not close to a church or their common community where bishops were their spiritual directors, *spiritual fathers* were called to lead them toward their own unique vocation. The spiritual director spent one on one time with the directees, who were at that time nuns and monks helping them to listen to the Holy Spirit and to nourish not only their spirits but their whole person. As a result the spiritual director became their confessor, their counselor, and their intimate friend.

The spiritual director should always be called to this vocation. They should hold all communication with the directee in total confidence. As a Roman Catholic priest holds all confessions in absolute confidence, so should a spiritual director keep everything told to them in a locked box safe in their heart.

A spiritual director cannot impart something to a directee that he does not possess himself. Therefore a director should be a person who lives a Rule of Life that includes prayer, meditation, journal keeping, and dream work. He should be of high moral character and be faithful to church attendance and to receiving communion on a regular basis. Above all he should be filled with the Holy Spirit and be a believer in God's Holy Word. He should be able to quote scripture and to admonish with scripture those directees who have gotten *off track*. He should be anointed for this unique work and should have hands laid on him and sent forth by his pastor or priest or elders to be a spiritual director.

A spiritual director is not a psychological counselor, he is a spiritual counselor. Therefore, he must faithfully read the Bible and know it. He should also read spiritual books by the saints of the church and other church leaders. He should be able to gently admonish his directees and remind them what God says in every situation. Praying with directees is also part of the job. In all situations pertaining to the soul the spiritual director should be an expert. If directees are expected to keep a journal, then the director should lead them in how to keep a journal. That discipline is an important part of the spiritual direction process.

Agreed upon dates and times should be set for the meetings between director and directee. The directee should come to the meeting prepared to share his journal and his dreams. The meeting should start with prayer and end with prayer. The Holy Spirit should be invited to the meeting. The goal of the director is to encourage, admonish, and gently lead the directee toward God and to hearing His voice.

Look around your church. Do you see a man or woman who is genuinely spiritual? Are they always willing to pray for others? If you want to hear from God about a special problem in your life, are they the first one you want to call? Is it a well-known fact at church that this person never tells what they know? Hopefully you know someone like that. They may or may not know anything about spiritual directors. Maybe they have never heard of such a concept. It might be helpful to pass this book on to them. It might open their eyes to a vocation they know nothing about.

In the future, churches would be greatly helped if they added to their programs of evangelism, missions, and outreach, programs of listening to God through prayer, meditation, worship, and dreams. Programs of learning to keep journals would be helpful. Classes specifically for possible vocations as spiritual directors would be useful. Along with classes about hospital visitors or neighborhood evangelism, there should be classes about interior work and drawing nearer to God. Anointed worship classes should be a part of this new way of thinking and teaching at church also. This would not necessarily be a music class. But it would be about holy worship.

Christians want more than the ordinary way of doing church. They want a real experience with a real God. They're tired of programs about reaching the neighborhood or feeding the hungry. Those are necessary and worthy jobs for the church. But Christians want more.

They want what Jesus called the abundant life. It does include financial prosperity. But it also includes a rich life in general. Your life will be rich in knowledge. Rich in signs, wonders, and miracles. Rich in the assurance that they are on the right road to becoming what God intends for them to be. How are we going to know those things unless we hear from God?

## Decision Time—What You Need to Do For Yourself

Whatever reason there was for you to have this book in your possession, I pray that it will make a difference in your life. If it doesn't speak to you now, and you toss it aside, I pray that someday, when you're ready to receive it, you'll pick it up and seriously read it again. May you put the suggestions into practice and find yourself closer to God than you ever imagined.

For those of you who read the book with an open heart and an eagerness to begin having a real experience with God, I commend you. For you, there is something to do, not tomorrow, but today. For you, today is the day to get started down the path to a closer relationship with God. The path begins with a decision—a decision to want God more. A decision to go after Him. A decision to search for Him with all of your heart (Jeremiah 29:13).

After that decision has been made and planted firmly within your mind and heart, then it's time to buy a journal. There are many journals in the Christian bookstores, office supply stores, and bookstores. Buy whatever draws you to it. If you like flowers, buy a floral one. If you like leather, then buy the one that feels good in your hands. Get one you love. If you love it, you'll use it. You won't mind carrying it around with you. You'll treasure it, and you'll make it your friend.

After you have made your purchase and taken it home, find a quiet place to be alone and undisturbed. Make a delicious drink and put your feet up. Relax and begin. This is a divine appointment. On the first page write your name and the date, include the day of the week. That is important for when you begin to see patterns in your life of when you do things. Under your name and date write the following scriptures: "Write all the words which I have spoken to you in a book" (Jeremiah 30:2), and, "Set up for yourself road marks, place for yourself guideposts; direct your mind to the highway, the way by which you went" (Jeremiah 31:21). These scriptures are reminders to you of why you are keeping a journal. Now you are ready to begin.

Remember first and foremost that your journal is a dream journal. Your dreams live on in the pages of your book. If you don't write them down, they disappear. Refer often to chapter three to remind yourself about how to keep your dream journal. Duplicate your Dream Interpretation Sheet and use it when working on the meaning of your dreams. It is a useful tool in the figuring- out process.

In addition to dreams your free-thinking journal entries should, of course, go into your journal. Also any doodles that you draw, any drawings of your dreams, and any plans you may have to create larger art projects.

If your dreams motivate you to start a business, add those plans. If you write poetry, they belong in your journal. If you have written conversations with God, family, or friends, add those.

In other words, if you think of anything that pertains to your life that means something to you, write it in your journal. If you find later that it doesn't mean anything, then you don't have to keep it. But sometimes it is difficult to know at the moment what means something and what doesn't. Sometimes it takes the passing of time and the certain knowledge of who you are and where you are going to know what to hold onto and what to let go of.

You will learn over time that God is speaking to you in more ways than you know. After you keep a journal for at least a year, you will able to go back, flip through the pages of your journal, and see where God has led you. Only from a distance sometimes can we see what previously was right before our eyes. In reviewing our journal we begin to pick up on patterns in our dream life. We see repeating symbols. We see repeating times and dates when we dreamed of certain events or certain people. After several months, a picture begins to form of our life and how God has brought us through emotional turmoil or bad habits. We begin to see that God had His hand on us when we may have not seen it with our eyes at the time. God begins to take shape on the pages of our journal where we had failed to see Him working in our lives day-to-day.

The more we see God on the pages of our journal, the more we want to see Him. We begin to hunger and thirst for Him and His Word. It is good to write scriptures on your journal pages that are especially meaningful. Talk about what they mean to you. Do they show up in your dreams? Are your dreams beginning to show you how they are healing you? Do certain events that used to upset you no longer bother you? Can you see that God is leading you beside still waters and restoring your soul? (Psalm 23:2-3).

Not only can God use dreams to heal you from the inside out. He can use a journal to do the same thing. There is something kinetic about the process of handwriting. The thoughts from your mind and heart, the messages moving down your arm, the motion of the writing, and seeing the words before your eyes are beneficial to the body. How? I don't know. I only know it works. Think of keeping a journal as good medicine for your soul. Add your understanding to that understanding, and you cannot fail to receive blessing upon blessing for your efforts.

## What You Need to Do for Others

After you begin to keep a journal and you grow comfortable with dream work, it is time for you to spread the good news. Spend time in prayer and ask God what He would have you do with the newfound knowledge and experience you have acquired. Perhaps God has something specific for you to do. If you have discovered new gifts and talents during this process, it's time to put them to work for the Lord. Other Christians need to know there is a way for them to draw nearer to God.

They need to know that God wants to speak with them in their dreams. Since many of them already are hungry for a powerful experience with the Lord, they are already receptive to what you have to say. If you find someone who isn't, then move on. God will eventually put someone open to Him in your path. That someone just might be your pastor or your priest. Meet with him, relate what you have discovered, and see if there is some way that this new knowledge can be put to work in your church. Believe me; you might not have to say anything to bring the subject up. By the time you are ready for this step, others will have already noticed a change in you. They may already be asking you what has happened to you. What has happened to light up your face like that? Why do you seem so *alive* all of a sudden? There seems to be a quiet serenity about you. Or you seem more purposeful about everything now. "What can we do to have what you have?" they may ask.

You could give them a copy of this book. Ask them to read it and get back to you with their questions. Or you could simply meet them for coffee and share your story. Tell them about what God is saying to you in your dreams. Tell them He wants to talk to them, too. And that they can also hear Him. If you are brave and trust that person, you might want to share something from your journal. Above all, be a witness. Relate to them that there is a better way to live. A hidden way, if you will. A life that is hidden under His wings (Psalm 91:4). There is a spiritual life to be lived here and now where revelation knowledge is passed to Christians while they sleep. All they need to do is pay attention and learn the symbolic language of God that He speaks to them in the night.

Tell them that God and Jesus Christ is the same, yesterday, today, and forever (Hebrews 13:8). And that He speaks to us through dreams just like He did to Joseph, Solomon, Paul, and others. He is doing now what He did then. He is healing, teaching, giving prophecies, and giving dreams. He has not changed. Tell them that you know it is true because it is happening to you.

You might be asked to speak to groups at church, or teach in a small group. You might be asked to start a journal group to share your dreams with close trusting friends. God can use you in any number of ways once you hear His voice and know what He is saying to you. He may give you something entirely new to do that hasn't been done before. You may choose to obey or not. I pray that you will. It is only by spreading this news that the church can recover its ability to hear God through dreams again.

## A Personal Numinous Dream

In the early 1990s I became seriously ill with adrenal failure, and I spent many weeks in bed and near death. As you can imagine I prayed constantly, and many Christian friends prayed also. As a result God healed me, and I recovered. But when I was at the lowest point I had a numinous dream.

> I was lying in bed, and Jesus came. He was wearing a white linen garment of one whole piece of cloth. It was dazzlingly white. He lay

> down beside me on my right side. He asked me, "Do you have your shield of faith?" I answered, "Yes." And I leaned over to the left side of the bed, and picked up a very large metal shield. It was gray metal and had a cross on the front. It was shaped like and looked like the shields of the Crusaders. I was surprised at how large the shield was and how light it was to lift. I had no problem picking it up. I lifted the shield from the floor with one hand and brought it over to us. It became as large as the king-sized bed. Jesus smiled. He said, "Cover us with your shield." And I did. I felt totally and completely safe under there with Jesus. His mouth was next to my ear, and He said, "Do you hear me speaking in your ear?" And I said, "Yes, Lord." And He faded away from my sight. He was no longer visible. And He said, "Do you still hear me?" I replied, "Yes, Lord." And then He became visible again and said, "Always remember this. Whether you see Me or don't see Me, I am here. I will speak to you, and you will hear me even if you can't see Me. I am always here. Will you remember that?" I answered, "Yes, Lord, I will always remember that." And I woke up.

Even now, as I write this dream again, the power of its effects overwhelms me—tears come, and I am thankful. As I said in chapter one, some dreams are so powerful they change your life forever.

If I had not written down the dream, would I have remembered it? Maybe, but I might not remember all of the details. And the details also bring me comfort and assurance. I am humbled that God would show me the size of my shield of faith (Ephesians 6:16). That dream image still fortifies me when doubt comes against me, and I need strengthening in my faith. From the whiteness of Jesus's linen garment to the electric feeling of His nearness to my ear to the sound of His whispering in my ear, all the details are still as fresh as they were the next morning after the dream. At a crisis in my life when I needed Jesus the most, He came to me in a dream.

He will do the same for you, for He is our Healer, Comforter, and Counselor. When you need Him the most in your life, He is there. Whether you can see Him or not see Him, it doesn't matter; He is there. He will speak to you and tell you what you need to hear. Like me, He might show up in a dream. Please welcome Him, and when He comes, draw near.

Sweet dreams.

# Charts

## Angels in Revelation

| | |
|---|---|
| Angel of the Lord | Rev 1:1 |
| Angel | (red letters) Rev 1:13-20, Rev 3:22 |
| Strong angel | Rev 5:2 |
| Many angels around the throne | Rev 5:11 |
| Four angels at the four corners of the earth | Rev 7:1-Rev 9:14 |
| Angel with the seal of the living God | Rev 7:1 |
| All angels around the throne | Rev 7:11 |
| 7 angels who stand before God and given 7 trumpets | Rev 8:1 |
| The 7 trumpets: | |
| 1) Hail and fire mixed with blood | Rev 8:7 |
| 2) Great mountain burning with fire | Rev 8:8 |
| 3) Great star fell from heaven | Rev 8:10 |
| 4) 1/3 of sun, 1/3 of moon, 1/3 of stars were darkened | Rev 8:12 |
| 5) Bottomless pit opened, locusts came | Rev 9:3 |
| 6) 3 plagues kills 1/3 of mankind | Rev 9:15 |
| 7) The Kingdom of the Lord came on the world | Rev 11:15 |
| Angels with golden censer | Rev 8:3-4 |
| Angel of the abyss | Rev 9:11 |
| Strong angel clothed with cloud and a rainbow on his head | Rev 10:1, (10:8 with a book) |
| Angel standing on sea and on land | Rev 10:5, 10:8 |
| Michael and his angels waging war | Rev 12:7 |
| The dragon and his angels thrown down | Rev 12:7-9 |
| 1) Angel flying with eternal gospel | Rev 14:6 |
| 2) Angel "Fallen is Babylon" | Rev 14:8 |
| 3) Angel (unidentified) | Rev 14:9 |
| 4) Angel out of temple | Rev 14:15 |
| 5) Angel out of temple with sharp sickle | Rev 14:17 |
| 6) Angel with power over fire | Rev 14:18 |
| 7) Unknown | |

7 angels with 7 plagues Rev 15:1
also with 7 golden bowls Rev 15:7
The Bowls:
1) Loathsome and malignant sores on men with mark of the beast Rev 16:2
2) Poured into sea, became blood and killed the sea Rev 16:3
3) Rivers and springs of water became blood Rev 16:4
4) Sun to scorch men Rev 16:8-9
5) Throne of the beast Rev 16:10-11
6) The great river, the Euphrates, dried up - frogs that were demons Rev 16:12-16
7) Upon the air, great earthquake, destruction of creation/ earth Rev 16:17-21
Later one of these angels showed John the New Jerusalem Rev 21:9
Angel of the waters Rev 16:4
Strong angel took up a stone Rev 18:1
Angel standing in the sun calling to birds Rev 19:17
Angel carrying key to the abyss, bound the dragon and serpent (Satan) for 1,000 years Rev 10:1
Angel - one of the 7 angels with bowls and plagues shows the bride Rev 21:9
12 angels at the 12 gates in the New Jerusalem Rev 21:12
Angel with the gold measuring rod Rev 21:15
Angel showed the river of life Rev 22:1
Angel of the Lord Rev 22:6

# Breastplate of High Priest - Exodus 28:16-20

Onyx stones engraved with names of the sons of Israel

Breastpiece was square, folded double

4 rows of stones on it

1) ruby (red), topaz (blue/purple), emerald (green)

2) turquoise (blue/green), sapphire (dark blue), diamond (clear)

3) jacinth (brown), agate (gray & white), amethyst (purple)

4) beryl (brown), onyx (black), jasper (green or reddish brown)

The stones in the ephod corresponded to the tribes of Israel

Exodus 39:10-13

Row 1) Reuben, Simeon, Levi

Row 2) Judah, Issachar, Zebullun

Row 3) Dan, Naphali, Gad

Row 4) Asher, Joseph, Benjamin

# Colors in Revelation

| | |
|---|---|
| God on throne - jasper stone and a sardius | Rev 4:3 |
| Rainbow - emerald green | Rev 4:3 |
| Golden crowns | Rev 4:4 |
| Horses: 1) White | Rev 6:2 |
| 2) Red | Rev 6:4 |
| 3) Black | Rev 6:5 |
| 4) Ashen (pale) | Rev 6:8 |
| Robes - white | Rev 6:11, 7:13 |
| Sun - black | Rev 6:12 |
| Moon - blood (red) | Rev 6:12 |
| Blood of the Lamb (red) | Rev 7:14 |
| Golden censer | Rev 8:3 |
| Golden altar | Rev 8:3 |
| Hail and fire mixed with blood (red) | Rev 8:7 |
| Green grass - burned up (black) | Rev 8:7 |
| Mountain (black) burning with fire (red, yellow), 1/3 of sea blood (red) | Rev 8:8 |
| Crowns on horses (gold) | Rev 9:7 |
| Golden altar | Rev 9:13 |
| Riders of the horses - breastplates color of fire (red, yellow) and of hyacinth (scarlet, blue, yellow) and of brimstone (yellowish) | Rev 9:17 |
| Idols - gold, silver, brass, stone, wood | Rev 9:20 |
| Strong angel - cloud (white), rainbow (various), sun (red, yellow), fire (red, yellow) | Rev 10:1 |
| Waters into blood (red) | Rev 11:6 |
| Red dragon | Rev 12:3 |
| White cloud | Rev 14:14 |
| Golden crown | Rev 14:14 |
| Golden girdles | Rev 15:6 |
| Golden bowls | Rev 15:7 |

| | |
|---|---|
| Scarlet beast | Rev 17:3 |
| Woman in purple and scarlet with gold and a gold cup | Rev 17:4 |
| Cargoes of gold | Rev 18:12-13 |
| Linen | Rev 18:16 |
| White horse | Rev 19:11 |
| Armies | Rev 19:14 |
| White throne | Rev 20:11 |
| Clear jasper | Rev 21:11 |
| Fountain stones | Rev 21:15 |
| City was pure gold, like clear glass | Rev 21:18 |
| Material of the wall, jasper | Rev 21:18 |
| Gates | Rev 21:21 |
| Streets | Rev 21:21 |

# Daniel: Symbols and Angels

Daniel 2:22 - ask God about your dreams

Daniel 2:28 - God reveals mysteries...

Daniel 2:30 purpose – that you may understand the thoughts of your mind

Daniel 2:38 - king = head of gold

Daniel 2:38 - 2nd kingdom = silver

Daniel 2:39 - 3rd kingdom = bronze

Daniel 2:40 - 4th kingdom = iron

Daniel 2:41 - divided kingdom = feet & toes = clay & iron

Daniel 2:44 - kingdom of God = Jesus' kingdom

Daniel 2:45 - the stone = Jesus

Daniel 2:47 - even Nebuchadnezzar admits that God is a revealer of mysteries

Daniel 3:25, 28 - angel in the furnace

Daniel 4:13 - angelic watcher

Daniel 4:20-22 - the tree = Nebuchadnezzar

Daniel 5:5 - the handwriting on the wall

Daniel 6:22 - angel that shut lion's mouth

Daniel 7:3-8 - Four Beasts

- Lion with wings of eagle, two feet like a man, with human mind
- Bear - three ribs in its mouth - told to devour meat
- Leopard - four wings of bird - had four heads - was given dominion
- Terrifying, strong animal with large iron teeth - ten horns (Daniel 7:24 - 10 kingdoms with 10 kings) - another little horn - three of the ten horns pulled out by the roots - little horn had eyes of a man and mouth very boastful - body destroyed (7:11) and given to burning fire

Daniel 7:9 - Ancient of Days - God the Father

Daniel 7:9 - throne with fiery wheels

Daniel 7:10 - river of fire

Daniel 7:10 - thousands upon thousands of angels
Daniel 7:10 - myriads upon myriads of angels
Daniel 7:13-14 - Jesus presented to the Father
Daniel 7:16 - told interpretation of dream
Daniel 7:17 - Four kings

- Jehoakim
- Nebuchadnezzar
- Belshazzar, son of Nebuchadnezzar
- Darius, the Mede & Cyrus the Persian

Daniel 7:21 - waging war with the saints and overpowering them
Daniel 7:23 - devour the whole earth, tread it down and crush it
Daniel 8:3 - dream #2

- ram 2 horns, one larger
- male goat, not touching (8:5-8) the ground, horn between his eyes - hit the ram and shattered his 2 horns
- horn broken replace by 4 horns
- Satan - small horn out of one of the four caused some hosts to fall and some stars to fall - called itself equal to Commander host - angels (8:9-12)
- some of the host - bad angels who fell
- Commander of the host - God

Daniel 8:13 - 2 angels discussing the holy place
Daniel 8:15 - angel who looked like a man
Daniel 8:16 - Gabriel can give understanding of visions
Daniel 8:20 - ram with 2 horns = kings of Mede & Persia
Daniel 8:21 - male goat = kingdom of Greece - large horn between eyes = 1st king
Daniel 8:22 - broken horn and the 4 horns = 4 kingdoms that will arise from his nation - oppose Prince of Princes (Jesus)
Chapter 9 goes back to king Darius chapter 6 - Medes = Chaldeans
The Throne of the Lord = Jerusalem Jeremiah 3:17
Daniel 9:24 - seventy weeks = seventy sevens
Daniel 10:1 - Cyrus, king of Persia
Daniel 10:4 - by the Tigris = the great river

Daniel 10:5 - man (angel) = heavenly messenger, belt pure gold, body like beryl (brown), Vision of Jesus, face like lightening, eyes, flaming torches, arms & feet bronze, sound of his words like sounds of tumult (Rev 1:12-16)
Daniel 10:9 - fainted
Daniel 10:13 - angel, prince of kingdom of Persia
Daniel 10:13 - chief prince
Daniel 10:16 - angel, looked like human, touched Daniel to speak
Daniel 10:18 - angel touched Daniel to be strengthened
Daniel 10:20 - angel, prince of Greece
Daniel 10:21 - angel Michael, prince of Israel
Daniel 11:2 - 3 kings arise, one rich king goes against Greece
Daniel 11:16, 41 - the Beautiful Land = Israel
Daniel 11:20 - Jewel of his kingdom = Jerusalem
Daniel 11:22 - prince of the covenant
Daniel 11:28, 30, 32 - holy covenant
Daniel 12:5 - 2 angels on bank of river, one dressed in linen, above the waters

---

# DREAMS IN THE BIBLE

| Scripture: | Dream: | Type: |
|---|---|---|
| Gen. 20:1-7 | Abimelech's warning dream | Warning dream |
| Gen. 28:12-15 | Jacob's glimpse of heaven<br>Promises of God given | Numinous dream |
| Gen. 31:24 | God told Laban not to speak to Jacob | Warning dream |
| Gen. 37:5-11 | Joseph's two dreams about the sheaves and the sun, the moon and the eleven stars | Prophetic dream |
| Gen. 42:6 | Fulfillment of Joseph's two dreams | |
| Gen. 40:5 | The cupbearer and the baker's dreams. Each person has his own dreams & own interpretation | |
| Gen. 40:8 | Interpretation belongs to God | |
| Gen. 40: 9-13 | Cupbearer's dream of Pharaoh's cup | Prophetic dream |
| Gen. 40:16-19 | Baker's dream about birds and basket | Prophetic dream |
| Gen. 41:1-7 | lst dream: Pharaoh's cow dream<br>2nd dream: Pharaoh's grain dream | Prophetic dream<br>Prophetic dream |
| Gen. 41:16 | It is not in me...God gives the answers | |
| Gen. 41:28 | Joseph interprets Pharaoh's dream about famine in Egypt | Prophetic declaration |
| Gen. 41:32 | Repeating of dreams | |
| Judges 7:13 | Gideon overhears a dream of the enemy and is encouraged | Prophetic dream |
| Judges 7:15 | Gideon worshiped God, then led the people in victory | |
| Kings 3:5-14 | God blesses Solomon through a dream | Blessing dream |
| Kings 9:1-9 | God reiteration of Davidic Covenant | Promise dream |
| Dan. 4:5 | King Nebuchadnezzar's dream about the tree | Numinous & prophetic dream |
| Dan. 7:1 | Daniel wrote down his dream of the four beasts | Prophetic dream |
| Matt. 1:20 | Joseph's dream about marrying Mary | Comforting, prophetic, & numinous dream |
| Matt. 2:12 | Magi's dream | Warning dream |
| Matt. 2:13-14 | Joseph's dream about fleeing to Egypt | Numinous, warning, & instructional dream |
| Matt.2:19-23 | Joseph's dream about returning to Israel | Numinous & instructional dream |
| Matt. 27:19 | Pilate's wife suffers with a dream about Jesus | Warning dream |
| John 1:51 | Jesus confirmed dream of Jacob when he was talking with Nathanael (Gen. 28:12) | |

## Hierarchy of Angels

First Sphere (Old Testament sources)
Seraphim
Cherubim
Thrones (Gr. Thronos) (New Testament sources)
Second Sphere (New Testament sources)
Dominions
Virtues
Powers
Third Sphere
Principalities
Archangels
Angels

# Symbols from Exodus and Other Books and Used in Liturgical Churches

Lamb - unblemished male - Ex 12:5-11
Bitter herbs - Ex 12:8
Blood on the doorposts - Angel of death passed over - Ex 12:13,22, 23
Leaven - symbol of sin - Ex 12:19-20, 1Cor 5:6-8
Unleavened bread - Ex 12:15,18, 19, 20 and Ex 34:25
Wine - The blood of the Lamb was a sign for the angel of death to pass by that house (Ex 12:21-23). Also the Covenant was ratified by blood (Ex 24:8) and the wine is the symbol for that blood. Jesus said the wine was His blood.
Holy water - symbol of God bringing the children of Israel through the Red Sea, escape from Death - Ex 14:Water - symbol of being "born again" - born through water to a new life - John 3:5
Manna - Ex 16:15, 31 and John 6:32-58
Ark of the Covenant - Ex 25:22
Bread of the Presence - Ex 25:30
Crosses - symbol of death, shed blood
Candles - Ex 25:31-40
Vestments - Ex 28
Altar - Ex 30:8
Incense - Ex 30:8
Ransom money - Ex 30:11
Holy Anointing oil - Ex 30:2
Ashes on forehead - humility of Abraham - Gen 18:27
Tabernacle - God speaking of himself - Jer 2:13
Gospel reading - Mt 28:19-20
Water - symbol of Noah surviving the flood - Peter 3:20 baptism - living water - John 4:10
Waters - peoples - Rev 17:15

Spring of water of life - Rev 21:6
River of life - Rev 22:3 22

---

# Symbols From Revelation

God's appearance on the throne - jasper stone and a sardius - Rev 4:3

Rainbow around the throne like an emerald - Rev 4:3

24 Thrones around the throne with 24 elders in white with gold crowns - Rev 4:4

Before the throne a sea of glass like crystal - Rev 4:6

7 horns and 7 eyes - 7 Spirits of God - Rev 5:6

Horses:

- White - conqueror - Rev 6:2
- Red - war - Rev 6:4
- Black - scales measuring/weighing - Rev 6:5
- Ashen (pale) - death with Hades following - Rev 6:8

White robes given to the martyrs - Rev 6:11, Rev 7:13, 14

Black as sackcloth (mourning) - made of hair (repentance) - Rev 6:12

Robes made white by the blood of the Lamb - Rev 7:14

Golden censer on golden altar - prayers of the saints - Rev 8:3

Locusts appeared like horses prepared for battle - Rev 9:7

200 million horsemen sent to kill 1/3 of mankind - Rev 9:15-21

Great red dragon - devil and Satan - Rev 12:3, 9

Song of Moses - Rev 15:3

Great harlot - is the great city - Rev 17:1-6, Rev 17:18

Great wealth - fine linen, purple, scarlet, gold, precious stones, pearls - Rev 18:16, 17

Fine linen - righteous acts of the saints - Rev 19:8

White horse carrying the King of Kings - eyes of fire, many crowns, - Rev 19:11

Armies clothed in fine linen, white and clean riding on white horses - the saints - Rev 19:14

Lake of fire - the second death - Rev 20:14

Brilliance of the New Jerusalem - very costly stone - crystal clear jasper - Rev 21:11

12 foundation stones of the wall with the 12 names of the 12 apostles of the Lamb - Rev 21:14

Gold measuring rod to measure the New Jerusalem - Rev 21:15

New Jerusalem - pure gold like clear glass - Rev 21:18

Foundations of the wall: Rev 21:19-20

- Jasper
- Sapphire
- Chalcedony
- Emerald
- Sardonyx
- Sardius
- Chrysolite
- Beryl
- Topaz
- Chrysoprase
- Jacinth
- Amethyst

12 gates = 12 pearls, each a single pearl - Rev 21:21

Street - pure gold like transparent glass - Rev 21:21

Leaves of tree of life - healing of the nations - Rev 22:2

---

# Endnotes


1. Morton Kelsey, *Dreams: A Way To Listen To God* (New York: Paulist Press, 1978), 9.
2. Louis M. Savary, Patricia H. Berne, Strephon Kaplan Williams, *Dreams and Spiritual Growth* (Ramsey, NJ: Paulist Press, 1984), 4.
3. Morton Kelsey, *Dreams: A Way To Listen To God* (New York: Paulist Press, 1978), 32-33.
4. Morton Kelsey, *God, Dreams, and Revelation* (Minneapolis: Augsburg Publishing, 1968), 231.
5. Keith Clark, Capuchin, *Make Space, Make Symbols* (Notre Dame: Ave Maria Press, 1979), 86.
6. Ibid 87.
7. Morton T. Kelsey, *The Other Side of Silence* (Paramus, N.J.: Paulist Press, 1976), 209.
8. Ibid 165-166.
9. Morton Kelsey, *Dreams: A Way To Listen To God* (New York: Paulist Press, 1978), 80.
10. Ibid 7.
11. Ward Hill Lamon, *Recollections of Abraham Lincoln 1847-1865* (Lincoln: University of Nebraska Press, 1994), 116-117.
12. *Merriam-Webster's Collegiate Dictionary*, Tenth Edition (Springfield, MA 1993).
13. A. J. Gordon, *How Christ Came to Church: A Spiritual Autobiography* (New York: Fleming & Revell Company), 63.
14. *Dreams and Dreaming* (Alexandria, VA: Time-Life Books, 1990), 137.

15. Robert L. Van de Castle, Ph.D., *Our Dreaming Mind* (New York: Random House, 1994), 14-15.
16. John A. Sanford, *Dreams: God's Forgotten Language* (New York: Crossroad Publishing, 1968), 63-64.
17. J. Baylis, *Sleep On It!* (Marina del Rey, CA: De Vorss and Co., 1977).
18. James Ryle, *A Dream Come True* (Orlando, FL: Creation House, 1995), 158-159.
19. Ibid 159-160.
20. W. Kaempffert, *A Popular History of American Invention* (New York: Scribners, 1924).
21. *Josephus Complete Works*. (Grand Rapids: Kregel Publications, 1981), 243-244.
22. Ralph L. Woods, *The World of Dreams* (New York: Random House, 1947), 362.
23. Maymie Kyrthe, *All About Christmas* (New York: Harper & Brothers, 1954).
24. James Ryle, *A Dream Come True* (Orlando, FL: Creation House, 1995), 126.
25. Hans Lietzmann, *A History of the Early Church* (Cleveland: The World Publishing Company, 1961, Vol. III) 75.
26. Lactantius XLIV, *Of the Manner in Which the Persecutors Died*, The Ante-Nicene Fathers, op. cit, VII, 318.
27. Eusebius, *Church History*, IX.9.
28. Louis M. Savary, Patricia H. Berne, and Strephon Kaplan Williams, *Dreams and Spiritual Growth*, (Ramsey, N.J.: Paulist Press, 1984), 103.
29 Reported in Lloyd Lewis, *Myths after Lincoln* (New York: Grossset & Dunlap 1957) p. 294. The story is told by Ward Hill Lamon, Lincoln's bodyguard and, later, biographer.

30. Gloria Fisher. *Living Here and There*. "My Holy Dream." Unpublished.
31. B. Kedrov. *Voprosy Psiologii 3*. "On the Question of Scientific Creativity" (1957), 91-113.
32. Merriam-Webster Online. http://merriam-webster.com/dictionary/symbol.
33. http://www.fundamentallyreformed.com. Bob Hayton. "Welch's Grape Juice, Worldly, Wisdom, and Wine." August 3, 2006.
34. Rev. J. D. Krout. "The Individual Communion Cup." United Brethren Review 17:2 (March-April 1906) 101-105.
35. http://www.welchs.com/about-welchs/history
36. http://www.eliyah.com/strongs.htm
37. http://en.wikipedia.org/wiki/Strongs_concordance
38. Charles Spurgeon, Metropolitan Tabernacle Pulpit (Carlisle, PA: The Banner of Truth, 1991) vol. 14, 217-228.
39. Morton Kelsey, *God, Dreams, and Revelation*, (Minneapolis, MN: Augsburg, 1974), 237.
40. *Book of Common Prayer*, Revised 1979. (New York: The Church Hymnal Corporation), 833.
41. http://www.catholic.org/saints/saint.php?saint_id=50
42. Web site www.salesians.org
43. Terry Matz 1996-2000, *St. John Bosco*. Catholic Online. http://catholic.org.
44. Saint John Bosco: Mission to Love. Movie, 2004.
45. Paul Kengor, *God and Ronald Reagan–a spiritual life*, (New York: HarperCollins, 2004), 157.

46. Ibid, 160.
47. James Robison, *Thank God, I'm Free*, (Nashville: Thomas Nelson, 1988),146-147.
48. John A. Sanford, *Dreams: God's Forgotten Language*, (New York: Crossroad Publishing, 1982), 59-60.
49. Ibid, 60.
50. Religious Experience and Journal of Mrs. Jerena Lee. http://www.umilta.net/jarena.html
51. Ibid. http://www.umilta.net/jarena.html
52. Revival Ministries International, *Rodney Howard-Browne*, http://www.revival.com
53. Paul Halsall, *Eusebius: The Conversion of Constantine*, http://www.fordham.edu
54. Eusebius Pamphilius, *The Life of the Blessed Emperor Constantine.*
55. Bill Johnson, *Dreaming With God*, (Shippensburg, PA: Destiny Image Publishers, 2006), 76.
56. Kenneth E. Hagin, *The Believer's Authority*, (Tulsa: RHEMA Bible Church, 1984), 8-9.
57. Catherine Marshall, *A Man Called Peter.*
58. http://en.wikipedia.org/wiki/Saint_Augustine
59. J. R. Hyland, "The Pope and the Homeless Cats: John Paul II Had a Dream," http://www.jesusveg.com/popecats.html
60. Catherine Marshall, *Something More*, (New York: McGraw-Hill, 1974), 97.
61. The Promise of Persecution. Greg Laurie. http://www.crosswalk.com/spirituallife/11577658.
62. NNDB. St. Ambrose. http://wwwnndb.com/people/558/000097267/

63. Gregory of Nyssa. Department of Internet Ministries. http://www.icono-grams.og/sig.php?eid=379
64. The Dream Encyclopedia. Tertullian. http://www.answers.com
65. The Dream Encyclopedia. Synesius. http://www.answers.com/topic/synesius-of-cyrene#ixzz1G2USUAUU
66. Catholic Online. St. Jerome Doctor of the Church. http://www.catholic.org/saints.
67. Michael H. Hart, *The 100: A Ranking of the Most Influential Persons in History*, (New York: Hart Publishing Company, 1978), 105-198.
68. Robert L. Van de Castle, Ph.D., *Our Dreaming Mind*, (New York: Ballantine Books, 1994), 80-81.
69. Morton T. Kelsey, *God, Dreams, and Revelation*, (Minneapolis: Augsburg Publishing House, 1968), 174-175.
70. Robert L. Van de Castle, Ph.D., *Our Dreaming Mind*, (New York: Ballantine Books, 1974), 89.
71. Meng Heinrich and Ernst Freud, eds., *Psychoanalysis and Faith*, (New York: Basic Books, Inc., 1963), 63, 110.
72. (*Psychoanalysis and Faith*, op. Cit., 104.)